Tuning the Guitar

THE SCIENCE AND THE ART

Tuning the Guitar

THE SCIENCE AND THE ART

Published by Amarilli Books

Copyright © 2016, Brian Capleton PhD

briancapleton.com

First Edition 2016

ISBN 9780993537233

A CIP catalogue record for this book is available from the British Library.

Brian Capleton PhD is an alumnus of Wolfson College Oxford, the Royal College of Music, Trinity College of Music London, Dartington College of Arts, and Keele University. He was for many years a Lecturer at the Royal National College where he taught piano tuning and technology.

Other books by the author include *Theory and Practice of Piano Tuning*, *Piano Action Regulating*, and *Studies in Musical Science and Philosophy* Vols. 1-4.

Preface

Every guitar is unique, and there is not just one technique for tuning a guitar. However, there are some universal principles that are the same in all cases.

There are secrets hidden in the principles of musical intervals and vibrating strings, which when understood can make the difference between really good tuning, and results that are unsatisfactory, compromised, or even just random.

If we know the secrets, and practise listening, we can expect to be much more in control of the result, just as an artist who understands the principles of colour and perspective, is much more in command of a painting.

Not everyone considers fine-tuning issues. Not everyone is concerned about the beauty of really good harmony. But if you are, then you will probably have already noticed that simply tuning guitar strings to notes on a keyboard, or a tuning meter, or by the basic 5th and 4th frets method, or even by harmonics, doesn't always give a satisfactory result, in the music you actually play.

There are very good reasons for this, that this book explains. The book is a route into understanding what all the issues actually are, and how to deal with them. And that means how to always get the result you want, by ear, in an efficient and expert manner.

Contents

Parts of the Guitar   11

The Basics   13

Harmonics   21

Tuning by Harmonics   26

The Background Story   35

Overview of the Issues   38

Beating and Adjacent Strings   40

Types of Intervals   47

Temperament   54

Stopping Sharp   67

Practical Points to Remember   73

Estimating Beat Rates   78

On Random Adjustments   81

Equal Temperament Tuning   85

Equal Temperament in Tablature   112

Non Standard Pure Tunings   118

The 2nd Fret Method   121

Parts of the Guitar
referred to in the book

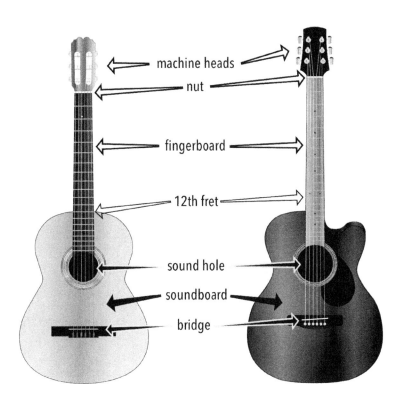

machine heads

nut

fingerboard

12th fret

sound hole

soundboard

bridge

The Basics

We are going to be talking about the tuning of a six-string guitar, tuned in the conventional way:

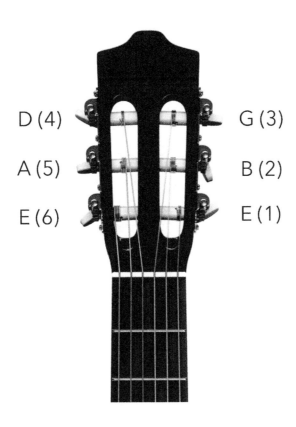

D (4)   G (3)

A (5)   B (2)

E (6)   E (1)

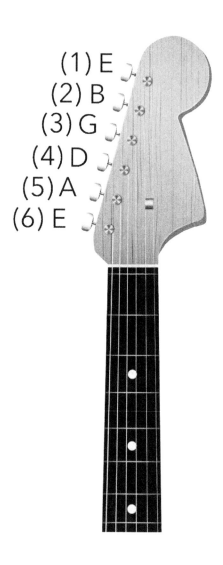

(1) E
(2) B
(3) G
(4) D
(5) A
(6) E

The numbers in brackets are the string numbers. So the 1st string is the highest-pitch E string, which is two octaves above the lowest-pitch E, or 6th string.

As notes on the piano keyboard, these notes (by string number) would be:

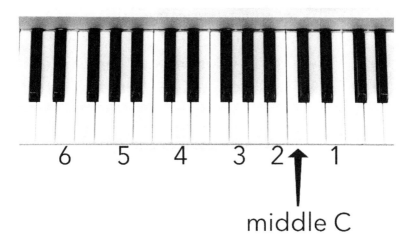

Section of a keyboard showing the corresponding string numbers of the guitar

The "musical distance" or pitch difference between any two notes is their *musical interval*. Musical intervals are named according to the number of steps in a scale, between the two notes.

We generally count *including* the first and last notes, so we can see in the picture that the musical interval between most adjacent strings, is **four** white notes on the keyboard, except for strings 2 and 3, where there are **three** notes.

So the musical interval between most adjacent strings on the guitar is called a *perfect fourth* (4 notes).[1]

The interval between the 3rd and 2nd strings, G and B, is a *major third* (3 notes). In this book we're not going to get into the full music theory behind these terms, but we need to know them, because we'll need to refer to them.

So to reiterate: The strings are tuned with a *perfect fourth* between adjacent strings, but the exception is the *major third* between the 3rd and 2nd strings (the G and the B).

On the keyboard, as shown above, a semitone is the musical distance between any one note, and the next adjacent note, whether black or white. On the guitar, it's the musical distance between adjacent frets on any string.

To count semitones we count the number of semitone *steps*, and *don't* include the note we start on. You can see on the keyboard that there are 5 semitones in each *perfect fourth*, and 4 semitones in the major third.

On the guitar, the 2nd and 3rd strings are B and G, which are a *major third* apart. So because there are *4* semitones in a major third, stopping the G string (3rd string) on the *4th* fret, also gives the note B, the same note as the B string.

Similarly, stopping the other strings, on the *5th fret*, will give the note of the next string up, tuned a perfect fourth above.

There are some other useful terms we need to be familiar with, because we'll be using them. A string that's plucked

_____

[1] The reason the word *perfect* is used for these intervals comes from the Pythagorean tradition (from *c.*600 BCE). Pythagoras saw musical intervals as part of Divine perfection. He knew that a perfect fourth and a perfect fifth, together, made a perfect octave, and that behind this relationship was a mathematical perfection, which he also saw as Divine.

without using the frets, is called an *open string*. If we press behind one of the frets, to make a different note, that's called *stopping* the string, or a *stopped string*, and the note we produce is called a *stopped* note.

There's always a part of the string that vibrates and sounds, and other parts of the string that don't. They might do in a very subtle way, but we'll ignore that. The main part of the string that vibrates and creates the sound (which is then amplified by the belly or soundboard) is called the *speaking length* of the string. So when we stop a string on a fret, we shorten its *speaking length*.

The Fifth And Fourth Frets Tuning Method

So the stopping positions of the strings, that give the same note as the next string up (going from string No. 6 to string No. 1), look like this:

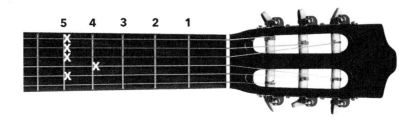

Tuning by Fifth and Fourth Frets

**Stopping positions giving notes matching the
next adjacent open string**

This is the most basic way of tuning a guitar: use the stopping positions to give the note of the next higher string. This is the method called *tuning by the fifth and fourth frets*. We will be referring to this again, later. It works, as a basic method, but it has drawbacks. The first drawback is that it is not possible to stop the string with the left-hand, and use the left hand to turn machine head and tune the string, at the same time.

Many guitarists overcome this problem by using the method of *tuning by harmonics*, which we'll come to shortly. The other disadvantage of the frets method, is that the tuning achieved is simply too ambiguous. You might think it would be highly accurate, but there are many reasons why it is not, no matter how good your aural skills in tuning the unisons.

We'll also be looking at these reasons, in due course. They are basically the same reasons why tuning all six open strings of the guitar, using an electronic tuning meter, often also falls short of producing the best possible results.

The relationship between open string notes and stopped notes on a guitar is often affected by factors that are unique to the guitar, despite that different guitars have their fret positions designed according to exactly the same principles.

*

The Pitch Reference

Tuning by ear, in the way that we are going to do, generally requires taking the pitch of one string to begin with, from some reliable source such as tuning fork, or perhaps another instrument.

Tuning forks are still a good option. They are small, lightweight, and reliable, but it's worth investing in a good quality one rather than a cheap one.

If you do use a tuning fork, hold the base and strike one prong of the fork (in the direction towards the other prong of the fork) on a surface that is not too hard or brittle. You shouldn't produce a high-pitched ping when striking the fork, which you will, if the surface is too hard. Something like your own elbow bone, struck through clothing, is about right.

The sound produced by a tuning fork on its own is very quiet. So most people, after striking the fork, place the base on the bridge of the guitar, so that the sound is amplified by the soundboard.

This makes the sound much louder, but there is a payoff. The energy of the fork is drained from the fork much faster, so the sound doesn't last very long, and *decays* or dies away rather rapidly. Just holding the fork close to your ear provides enough sound without this energy drain.

(Another way sometimes used, to hear the sound loudly, *and* keep both hands free for playing strings and turning the machine-heads, is to hold the base of the tuning fork between your teeth. The sound from the fork travels directly through the bone to the ear, without such rapid energy drain. However, if you do this, there is *a risk of damage to yourself, or to the guitar, if you accidentally drop the fork* - so it is not recommended).

The most common tuning fork is for the note A, so that's the one we'll be referring to. The standard A tuning fork matches the first A above middle C, so that's actually higher than the pitch of the first string on the guitar.

However, we can still easily use it for tuning the 5th or 4th string. The reason is because guitar strings produce *harmonics*. That's what we'll talk about in the next chapter.

The standard first string for tuning is actually the D string, which tends to be more stable, and is more centrally placed across the compass of the open strings. The way in which we can tune the D string from an A fork, is something I'll be explaining.

Harmonics

Most guitarists would have heard of *harmonics*, because they sometimes form part of the music that guitarists play. They are rather beautiful sounds that are played by touching the string lightly at certain positions, and plucking the string. What *are* these harmonics?

Nearly all musical sounds are actually *recipes* of *sound ingredients*, cooked-up, so to speak, by whatever it is that is making the sound. In the case of the guitar, that's the strings in the first instance, and then the soundboard and body of the guitar.

The reason guitar strings have such a good musical sound, is because they produce *harmonics* as their ingredients. Harmonics are acoustical ingredients whose frequencies and musical pitches have a special, musical relationship to each other. It's this that gives the overall recipe of the sound they produce, a very distinct musical pitch.

Now as it happens, some sound engineers and scientists would probably argue that in guitar sound these ingredients shouldn't really be called *harmonics*, but rather, *partials*. We're not going to worry about this right now. We will come back to it though. It's just a matter of how accurate you are being.

Most guitarists refer to these sound ingredients as *harmonics*, so that's what we're going to call them for the time being. It's accurate enough, for now.

If you touch a string lightly, *directly over* the 12th fret - just touch it but don't push it down to the fret - and then while still touching the string, pluck the string not too far from the bridge, you'll hear a harmonic. *As soon as you hear the harmonic, you can take your left hand away from the string.*

Always, when sounding harmonics, if you can't hear a clear sound, then try plucking the string at a different position. The plucking point can enhance or suppress the sound of a harmonic.

It's a beautiful, etherial sound. What you are hearing is the *2nd harmonic* in a whole set that make up the ingredients for the sound of that string.[2]

Essentially, what you're doing by lightly touching the string directly over the fret (rather than slightly behind it, as you would for stopping string), is simply preventing most of the other ingredients (harmonics) from sounding, except this one. You're not introducing something that wasn't already there, in the sound of the open string. You're just making it show up, by removing most of the other ingredients.

If you just pluck an open string in the ordinary way, then all the harmonics sound together, mixed together in proportions of a recipe that depends on how you pluck the string, and where along the string you pluck it. Because they are all sounding together, it's not so easy to pick out any one. But you still can, just as you can often pick out individual ingredients in a food recipe.

Do the same now by touching the string over the *seventh* fret, and you'll hear the *third* harmonic. If you want to hear the first harmonic - sometimes called the *fundamental* -

---

[2] You may find that sometimes some people call this the first harmonic, or first *overtone*. We are calling it the second harmonic, because there is another harmonic lower in pitch than this one, the same as the musical pitch of the string when ordinarily plucked. If you were to analyse the sound of the string in sound engineering, you would find a series of harmonics, and the one that we hear when we touch the string at the 12th fret position is indeed the second in the series.

touch the string just where it comes off the nut, on the soundboard side of the nut.

The string-touching positions for the first six harmonics of any string, are as follows:

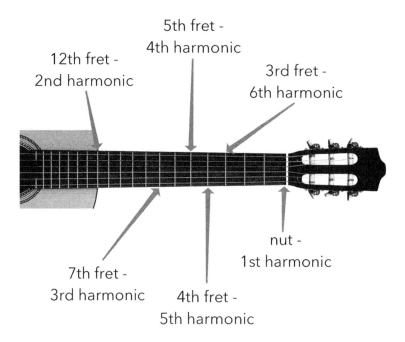

So on any string, you can run through the sequence of harmonics 1 to 6, for that string, in the order:

nut

12th fret

7th fret

5th fret

4th fret

3rd fret

You'll notice, if you do this, a musical pattern in the sequence. The pitches of the harmonics actually form the notes of a major chord.

The series of harmonics goes on, theoretically, infinitely. But in practice the harmonics become weaker and weaker the higher up the series they are.

If you analysed the sound of an open string in sound engineering, you would only normally ever be seeing harmonic numbers in double figures, before the strength of the harmonics disappears beneath the background "noise floor".

It's this orderly, musical arrangement of the harmonics - the ingredients of the tone of a string - that is the powerful influence behind beautiful, well tuned, harmony and musical intervals. It's also the reason that when harmony or musical intervals or not so well tuned, they don't sound so good.

Any open string note or any stopped note is a note whose tone consists of a unique recipe acoustically "cooked up" from these *harmonics* ingredients.

So when two notes are sounding together, there are two recipes sounding. It's the way the recipes match to each other, or not, as the case may be, that determines whether harmony or musical intervals sound beautifully in tune, or not.

Let's look at the A string - the 5th string. Its *harmonics* ingredients, up to the 5th harmonic, fall into the following pattern (*we're using standard guitar notation - the notes sound an octave lower than written*):

The first 5 harmonics of the open 5th string, the A string

The pitch of a standard A 440 tuning fork doesn't actually coincide with the normal musical pitch of the guitar's A string. Rather, it coincides with its 4th harmonic (It's at the pitch of the first A above middle C, on a piano keyboard).

So if we tune the A string to a standard A tuning fork, *it's at the pitch of that 4th harmonic* that the real business of what happens, takes place. Similarly, when we tune the D string to the A fork, we are tuning the D string's 3rd harmonic, which is at the same pitch as the fork. But we don't have to think about this. With a little ear training, we can just hear it naturally. We'll be talking about this more, soon.

Tuning by Harmonics

Probably the most popular way of tuning the guitar, after the frets method, is to use *harmonics*. Plucking harmonics only requires briefly and *lightly* touching the string *directly over* the 12th, 7th, or 5th fret (there are others, too) with the left-hand. *The string is not pressed down to the fret.* (There is of course a technique for doing it with the right hand, too).

Once the harmonic is sounding, you can take your hand away, and the harmonic will continue to ring on. This means that your left is free to alter the tuning of the string. This is the great advantage of the *tuning by harmonics* method.

We are going to go through this method now, into two different ways.

The guitar is designed for a tuning system called Equal Temperament. We're going to be talking about what that is, in due course. For now, we can think of it as very much to do the fact that the guitar has frets.

The frets on the guitar are all parallel and at right angles to the centreline of the fingerboard. And there is just one straight fret for all the strings that are stopped on that fret. Rather than having separate little frets for each string.

The only way we can achieve this with any degree of accuracy and efficiency, is to use this tuning system called Equal Temperament.

If you think of a musical interval as the musical distance between one note and another, then that musical distance is the "size" of that musical interval. Equal Temperament is a way of tuning musical notes so that the size of all the semitones is always the same. In other words, an octave is made up of 12 semitones, all of equal size.

Now you'll notice that on the guitar the distances between adjacent frets, which are also for notes a semitone apart, are not all the same. That's not because the semitones are different musical sizes, but because in order to get the semitones to be all the same musical size, the positions of the frets work out in that way. It's all a question of ratios, rather than fixed distances, but we don't need to get into that here.

The point is that in order to have nice straight, parallel frets, one for each semitone, we have to have all the semitones the same musical size, and when we are doing that, then we are using *Equal Temperament*.

So the guitar is designed for Equal Temperament. But the most popular way of tuning the guitar by harmonics, turns out to be a way that is inconsistent with what is necessary for Equal Temperament. It produces a particular kind of tuning on the guitar, that is *not* Equal Temperament. So it has its own characteristics, and its own problems.

So the first way we'll look at tuning by harmonics, is this most popular way. The fact that it's the most popular, however, doesn't mean it is necessarily the *best*.

The second way we'll look at tuning by harmonics, is a way that is consistent with Equal Temperament. However, that doesn't mean that it will solve all the tuning problems that guitarists often find in the tuning.

Standard Tuning by Harmonics

For this method we'll be using harmonics produced over the 5th and 7th frets. Remember that when you pluck a harmonic you can immediately take your left hand away from the string, and the harmonic will continue to ring on.

Harmonics over the 12th, 7th or 5th frets, will generally ring on long enough for you to move your hand to the machine head and tune the string.

Let's begin by assuming the D (4th) string is already in tune. Follow this in practice, and the pattern will be clear.

1. Pluck harmonics over the 7th fret of the D string, and the 5th fret of the A string.

2. Lower the A string a little and you should hear a "wahwah" sound in the combined harmonics. This is called *beating*.

3. Pluck the harmonics again and begin raising the A string. You will hear the speed of the beating slow down. If the harmonics become too quiet at any time, just pluck them again.

4. Continue to raise the A string until you hear the beating stop.

5. If you raise too far, the beating will start up again. If that happens you need to lower the A string again, and tune it up again.

6. Now use the tuned A string as your reference source, and begin tuning the E (6th) string. Now you take the harmonics over the 7th fret of the A string, and the 5th fret of the E string. Do the same thing again, first

lowering the E string, and then tuning it up until the beating disappears.

7. Now we tune the G string. This time, we are back to using the D string as a reference source. So we are taking 7th fret harmonic of the G string, and the 5th fret harmonic of the D string. Lower the G string and then tune it up until the beating disappears.

8. Now we tune the B string. The B string is the odd one out. We are going to use the E (6th) string as the reference source. Pluck the harmonic over the 7th fret of the E string, and just tune the open B string to this. Again, begin by lowering the B string, and then tuning it up until the beating stops.

9. Finally, we tune the E (1st) string. You *can* tune this by the same method, plucking the 7th fret harmonic over the E (1st) string, and the 5th fret harmonic over the B string. Alternatively, we can use the A string or the D (6th) as a reference source.

    Pluck the harmonic over the 7th fret of the A string, or the 5th fret of the D (6th) string, and just tune the open E (1st) string to the harmonic. Again, lower the E (1st) string, and then tune it up until the beating disappears.

Double check that everything is in order. If so, now let's now do some interval checks:

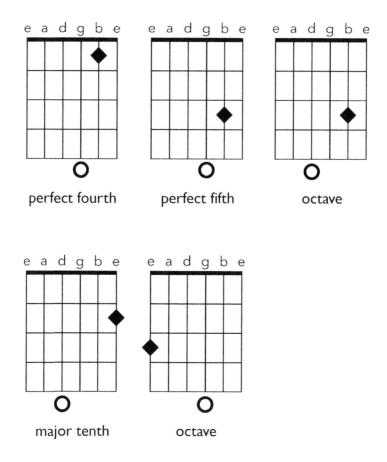

perfect fourth   perfect fifth   octave

major tenth   octave

Checks After Tuning by Harmonics

What you'll find is that all these intervals (and others, too), are left with questionable tuning. It is possible to become accustomed to the tuning of these resultant intervals, and not to really notice how mistuned they are.

Take the last check shown here, the octave G - G: Try retuning the 6th string. Start by lowering it considerably, and then listen to the harmonics (5th fret on the sixth (E) string, and 7th fret on the 5th (A) string), as you bring the string back up again. But this time, don't bring it all the way. Leave it a little flat, with the harmonics beating away, really quite fast, at around 4 beats every second. Now check the octave again, and you should find its tuning much improved.

Listen to that perfect fourth, between the open G string and the B string stopped on the 1st fret. Is that really a good tuning? Retune the G string by raising its tension just a little, listening to the major third between the G and the B string as you go. Notice the change to the major third, and then check again the perfect fourth. You should notice how much better it sounds.

That major tenth between the open D string and the 1st string stopped on 2nd fret, is actually quite coarsely tuned, with the F# way *too* sharp. Try lowering the first string a little, and listening to the major tenth again. You should find it sounds much sweeter.

Listen to that octave between the open D string, and the D stopped on the 3rd fret of the second string. It's not *really* an octave at all. Tweak up the open D string just a little, and you'll find the octave sounding much better.

At the root of these problems, and many others, is that we tuned all those harmonics until the beating disappeared. The guitar is designed for Equal Temperament tuning, and Equal Temperament demands that the these perfect fourths between the open strings are *not* tuned in this way.

We'll talk more about temperament and how it works, a little later. For now, let's just go through tuning by harmonics again, but this time taking into account the principles of Equal Temperament, in tuning those open perfect fourths.

*

The principle we are talking about, is that in Equal Temperament perfect fourths are tuned a little *wide*. Now the idea of intervals being *narrow* or *wide* is something we'll also talk more about, a little later. So don't worry too much about that for the purpose of this exercise. Just follow the instructions to get a feel for what happens.

Equal Temperament By Harmonics

1. We're going to start again on the D string. If you want to re-tune the D now to some external reference source, such as a keyboard, that's fine. To tune it to an A tuning fork, pluck the harmonic over the seventh fret, and tune until the beating disappears. If you focus your ear at this pitch, you can do this just by listening to the open string plucked in the normal way.

2. Now we are going to tune the A string, in the same way we did before, beginning by lowering the string to deliberately set it flat to start with. Pluck the harmonics again, and tune up the A string, but this time, paying careful attention, stop a little short of taking it all the way to the point where the beating disappears.

   We want to leave it beating slightly flat. Not enough that it sounds really bad, but enough that it is still definitely beating. It should be about one clear beat every 2 seconds.

   However, be absolutely sure that it is beating slightly *flat*, and that you haven't gone past the point where the beating disappears, and taken it slightly sharp. Once you start to go sharp with the string, it will start beating again. But it must be *flat*, and not sharp!

You just have to pay very careful attention as you bring the string up from too flat, and make sure you stop short of making the beating disappear.

3. Now using the A string as the reference string, we're going to do the same thing in tuning the E (6th) string. Leave it beating slightly flat by about the same amount.

4. Now it's time to tune the G string, but this time we are going to tune it very slightly *sharp*. So pluck the harmonics, and bring the string up from flat, until the beating disappears, and then deliberately go a *little* further, until beating just starts again.

   You may find it easier to set the string *sharp* to begin with, and then listening to the harmonics, lower it until the beating slows right down, but doesn't quite disappear. Either way, you have to be sure that the string is beating very slightly sharp, and not flat.

5. Now we can tune the B string as we did before, to the 7th fret harmonic on the E (6th) string. This is a unison, so we can tune it beatless.

6. Lastly, we can tune the E (1st) string in the same way we did before, with no beating. Either use the 7th fret harmonic on the A string, or if you like, just tune the double octave with the open sixth string.

You should now find that the open G - B sounds sweeter than it did when we tuned adjacent string harmonics beatless. Try testing the perfect fourth, and perfect fifth, shown in the tablature, again. These intervals too, should now sound much better. However, if you try some of the other intervals, you may find there is not so much success.

*

33

The method we have just used is probably the best all-round easy and quick method of tuning, consistent with Equal Temperament. It may be all you'll ever need. It is a much better overall result than "tuning out the beating" in the open string perfect fourths.

However, many guitarists still find themselves having to make further adjustments in order to get the tuning "right" according to the keys and chords that are being used.

Some of this is an attempt to make some musical intervals "better" than they are supposed to be in Equal Temperament. For example, tuning the open string perfect fourths until beating disappears, does create a nicer sounding interval than when you leave it still beating. But that also produces subsequent problems, because the guitar is designed for Equal Temperament tuning, and Equal Temperament demands that these perfect fourths should be left beating wide.

But also, much subsequent "tweaking" of tuning can be due to the fact that leaving the open perfect fourths beating in the way we just did, doesn't necessarily solve all tuning issues, especially if the strings are not in perfect condition.

So what we are now going to do, is look into all the issues, because once we understand them, we can control them, according to our needs.

The Background Story

The idea of Equal Temperament is that it doesn't favour the tuning in any key, at the expense of others, in the way that guitarists often do when tweaking the tuning.

But tuning by harmonics, leaving beating between the open string harmonics, in the way that we just tried it, doesn't necessarily give a result that is as close as possible to this principle of equal favour.

That's because although we followed *one* of the principles of Equal Temperament, that the perfect fourths should be beating a little wide, true Equal Temperament tuning actually requires a level of precision that we were not achieving. And it's not just about perfect fourths.

Not only that, but the level of precision that true Equal Temperament requires, *is not generally possible* just by tuning the open fourth harmonics of the guitar. There are reasons for this that we will be coming to shortly.

To put this in context, let's just mention something about Equal Temperament's history. Equal Temperament is just one of many temperament systems. *Something approaching it* can naturally *tend* to result on fretted instruments, because of the frets, but this doesn't happen on keyboard instruments. So it wasn't used for keyboard tuning (on pianos) until the mid 19th century.[3]

It wasn't until then that a method for accurately tuning it on keyboards was worked out. Before then, for about 400 years, keyboards were tuned to other temperaments altogether, or in the previous century by just very rough attempts at Equal Temperament.

In fact, for a long time, the business of playing fretted instruments, with their *roughly* Equal Temperament tuning, together with keyboard instruments, with at best, their *roughly* Equal Temperament, was a literally a laughing matter.[4] *Roughly* Equal Temperament - which is what you often get even on a modern guitar - leaves unresolved problems in the tuning.

Keyboard instruments can't just copy note by note, the tuning of fretted instruments, or *vice versa*. The *only* tuning system that in theory, can match well, both on a keyboard instrument, and on a fretted instrument, is accurate Equal Temperament.

Actually, even if you try tuning the guitar string by string, from the corresponding notes on a modern keyboard, which *is* tuned to accurate Equal Temperament, you might get a kind of reasonable result, but you *still* might find

---

[3] You'll sometimes hear that the composer JS Bach used it in the 18th-century. He wrote a set of preludes and fugues often referred to as "the 48", because there were 48 of them, covering all key signatures. Bach gave them the title *Das Wohltemperierte Klavier*, which means "The Well Tempered Keyboard Instrument". It is now well-known in musicology that this doesn't refer to Equal Temperament, but to another tuning system that allows pleasant playing in all keys, but nonetheless does favour some keys over others.

[4] There is a letter from Giovanni de' Bardi to Giulio Caccini from the late 1570s, to this effect. See Lindlay, Mark, *Lutes, viols and temperaments*, CUP, 1984, p. 44.

intervals on the guitar that aren't really satisfactory, for playing some solo guitar music.

It works the other way round, too. You couldn't successfully tune a piano satisfactorily, by simply copying notes off a guitar, however well tuned the guitar. Nor can you fine tune a piano simply by tuning perfect fourths, like we just did on the guitar. It often doesn't really work on the guitar, and it certainly doesn't work on the piano. This is because the acoustics of different strings and different soundboards is far more complex than we might think.

Expert piano tuners tune a mixture of major thirds and sixths, and tenths, as well as perfect fourths, perfect fifths, and octaves. If we want to tune good Equal Temperament on the guitar, then we pretty much have to apply the same kind of principle.

As it happens, the guitar has an open major third between the G and B strings. It also has an open the major sixth between the D and B strings. So when, a little later, we come to the method for tuning Equal Temperament on guitar, we're actively going to tune these intervals, rather than simply leaving their tuning to emerge from how we tune the open perfect fourths.

Overview of the Issues

Tuning the guitar using the 5th and 4th frets method is a basic way to start. However, guitarists often find that having done this, there are many finer details in the tuning of the guitar that subsequently arise, that are less than satisfactory.

When we are listening to the tuning of intervals such as octaves, perfect fifths, perfect twelfths (a perfect fifth plus an octave, which frequently occurs in guitar music) and major thirds, then we are not just hearing musical pitches.

The factor in the sound quality that tells us when an interval is sour, harsh, or sweet, in its intonation, is also largely due to *beating*, which we have already talked about. Basically, to reiterate, "beating" is a kind of *wahwah* modulation effect that happens in the sound. If the speed of the beating is too fast, it spoils the sound of the interval.

As musicians, if we are aware of good or poor tuning in musical intervals, then we are at least subliminally aware of beating. What we will be talking about later involves becoming consciously aware of it, and taking control of it.

Temperament

Many guitarists, as they become more familiar with tuning, understand that there is this thing called *temperament*, that affects the tuning of the guitar. Before realising this, some guitarists just assume that tuning problems arise because of imperfections in the guitar.

We are going to be looking in detail at what temperament is, and how to deal with it. Even if we are using the best guitar in the world, this issue of temperament still exists, and wields its effects.

However, it is not the case that all tuning issues on the guitar simply come down to the rules of temperament. Temperament is only one factor. There are other less well-known factors that can have a major effect on how we tune the guitar.

Stopping Sharp

One factor is called *inharmonicity*, which results from string stiffness. This usually gets worse, as the strings get older. It causes the harmonics to be displaced, upsetting the musical arrangement of them that we looked at. Generally, they become sharper. This results is an effect called *stopping sharp*. It means that a stopped note can sound sharper than it should, and when we tune by *beats*, the speed of the beating is affected.

False Beating

False beating is beating produced by a single string on its own, rather than by two strings that form a musical interval. It is generally slow beating, and occurs because the string is free to vibrate in more than one transverse plane. It confuses the issue of leaving deliberate beating in intervals, and leads to errors.

Beating and Adjacent Strings

Try stopping the 5th string, A, on the 5th fret. The stopped note should be a D, the same note as the open 4th string. Sounded together, they are two different strings playing the same musical note, which is called a *unison*.

If the interval between the open 4th and 5th strings is not in tune, then the unison will sound out of tune. It will *beat*. Make sure that the two strings are *not* in tune, by lowering the tension on the 5th string, and then gradually bring the tension in the 5th string back up, a little at a time, listening to the unison.

You'll notice that as the unison comes closer and closer to being in tune, there is the "wahwah" effect in the unison. This is *beating* again. Each "wah" in the sound is referred to as a *beat*.

When the strings are a long way out of tune, this *wahwah* effect, or *beating*, is fast. As the strings are brought into tune, the beating gets slower and slower. The unison is in tune when the beating stops altogether.

It's only when the strings are in tune, that the beating stops. If either string is either sharp or flat, it doesn't matter which, the beating will be there.

So the presence of beating in the sound of the unison can tell you how much the unison is out of tune, because the more it is out of tune, the faster it beats. If you're not already familiar with this, then it's worth practising listening and tuning, until you are very familiar with the effect.

The beating by itself can't tell you whether a string is sharp or flat. But you can deduce it easily enough. If you are tuning a *unison*, and raising the tension, and the beating is getting faster, then you know the string is too sharp. You need to lower the tension. If you are lowering the tension, and the beating is getting faster, then the string is too flat. You then need to raise the tension.

If you're tuning a *unison*, then you are always aiming to slow the beat down, and eventually, eliminate it, if you can.

A similar thing happens when tuning other musical intervals that are not unisons. We are now going to try this, in tuning the open 4th and 5th strings, D and A.

*

You might have guessed that we are going to be listening to *beating*. We are, but there's something else to talk about first. Now here, the first thing to watch out for, is an effect of *psychoacoustics*. This is to do with how our brain *interprets* sound signals coming into our ears. It's possible for certain illusions to happen, that are "built into" the way our brain interprets incoming sound.

If you detune the A string by setting it too flat, and then slowly bring it up again into tune, you should notice beating again, that becomes slower as the A string approaches a pure perfect fourth below the D string. The beating may seem slightly less clear than when we tuned the unison, but it is nonetheless perfectly audible. If you don't hear it to begin with, come back to it after reading on.

Now it may seem, that this beating is happening somewhere at the pitch of the a string of the A string or the D string. Both strings have quite a deep, "bass-like" sound, and it may seem like the beating itself is part of this quite deep tone of the two strings. But in fact, if it does sound like that to you, that's a psychoacoustic effect. Let's have a look at what is actually happening.

Let's look at the first five ingredients, or harmonics, of the open A string (the 5th string). Here they are, again using standard guitar notation (which means played on a keyboard, you would have to play the notes an octave lower to get the right pitch):

Now let's see this side-by-side with the first five harmonics of the D string (the 4th string):

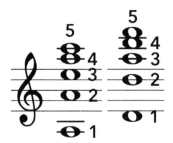

The first five harmonics of the open A string, together with the first five harmonics of the open D string

You'll notice that the 4th harmonic of the open A string is the same note as the 3rd harmonic of the open D string. Essentially, when the two strings are in tune, these two harmonics form a harmonic unison. It's *this* that actually creates the beating, when there is a mistuning between the 4th harmonic of the A string and the 3rd of the D string.

It's *at this musical pitch* that the beating actually happens. You can *hear* that musical pitch by plucking the harmonic over the 7th fret of the D string (or the 5th fret of the A string).

If the two open strings are tuned such that there is a well tuned perfect fourth between them, then essentially, what this means is that there is a well tuned perfect fourth between the *first harmonics of the strings*. (The first harmonic is also often called the *fundamental*).

When we tune a *pure* perfect fourth, the 4th harmonic of the open A string will be in good unison with the 3rd harmonic of the open D string - there will be minimal or no beating. This is precisely what we were doing when we tuned by harmonics to begin with.

So the second time we tuned by harmonics, and deliberately left the open string pair beating, we *weren't* tuning a *pure* perfect fourth. We were tuning a *tempered* perfect fourth.

A similar situation occurs with all open string adjacent pairs. There is one harmonic from each string, that coincides with one harmonic from the other string. (There is actually also another pair, higher in the harmonic series, sounding an octave higher). It is these *coinciding harmonics* that produce the beating.

Now let's try listening to this in practice.

Firstly, make sure that the A string is flattened a bit, so that the A and D strings are not quite in tune. Now just as we did before, pick out the relevant harmonics, and play them by touching the A string lightly over the 5th fret, and the D string over the 7th fret.

We're looking at the 4th harmonic of the A string, and the 3rd harmonic of the D string. Here they are:

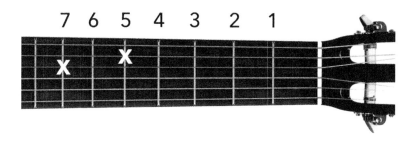

Finger touching positions to produce the two main harmonics that beat when tuning the open A and D strings

Lightly touching both positions at once, and plucking both strings, at once, will clearly sound the beating harmonic. It's the same one responsible for the beating heard when both open strings are played together. (You may also be able to hear the other beating harmonic an octave above this one, that beats twice as fast).

Familiarise yourself with the musical *pitch* and sound of the beating harmonic, and then just listen to the two open strings played together. You should still be able to hear this same beating harmonic within the sound of the two open strings. If you can do this, you are hearing the beating much more accurately when you play the two open strings, because you are *listening to the right pitch.*

You can repeat this exercise using the same fret numbers, in the same geometric pattern, for all the adjacent string pairs that have a perfect fourth between them. You should actually try this. The B and G, or 2nd and 3rd strings, is the exception, because the interval between them is a major third.

In the case of the 2nd and 3rd strings, the B and G, to isolate the beating harmonic, we would need to finger over the 4th fret on the 3rd string (G), and the 5th fret on the 2nd string (B):

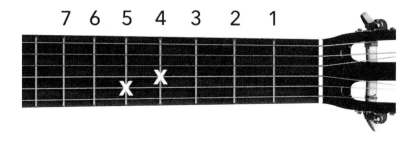

Finger touching positions to produce the two main harmonics that beat when tuning the open G and B strings

This one is often much more tricky for producing clear harmonics. In fact, once you have familiarised yourself with the musical *pitch* at which the beating happens, it is generally much more clearly heard when both open strings are plucked, then when trying to produce the harmonics separately.

This practise of listening to harmonics improves your ability to fine-tune adjacent open strings. Many guitarists actually play the harmonics themselves, by touching the strings lightly, when tuning adjacent strings. But you don't have to, if you train your ear, because those harmonics are already there anyway, in the sound of the open strings.

However, bear in mind that when we come to actually fine-tune the guitar, we are *not* necessarily going to tune these intervals between adjacent strings so that the beating disappears completely.

Types of Intervals

All the musical intervals that are available on the guitar fit together into a complex network.

But they *don't* fit together in the way that we perhaps would like them to, or expect them to, because of the natural acoustics of strings and musical intervals. The main issue in tuning or fitting together any musical intervals, is the principle of *temperament*.

The issue of temperament means that there are *rules* about how musical intervals should be tuned, or rather, deliberately *mis-tuned* slightly, in order for them to fit together. But it turns out, especially on an instrument such as the guitar, that there are also reasons why those rules themselves have to be "bent".

We don't need to get too deeply into the theoretical details of all this - all we need to do is to understand enough to be in command of fine tuning the guitar.

It turns out that most of the time, if we pay attention to just 5 kinds of musical interval, then we will be handling the situation well. If we get it right, all the other intervals will tend to fall into line by themselves, without too much bother. These 5 main musical intervals are:

- The octave
- The perfect fifth
- The perfect fourth
- The major third
- The major sixth

There are places, though, where we will be listening to the perfect twelfth, which is a perfect fifth plus an octave, and the major tenth, which is a major third plus an octave. We will also be listening to the double octave between the 1st and 6th strings.

This is the most important double octave on the guitar, and is a good place to start practising listening to beats. Start by tuning the 1st string with the 6th string. Begin by lowering the pitch of the 1st string, and then raising it back into tune, playing both strings at once, listening for the beating. Aim to eliminate the beating. Listen at the pitch of the 1st string.

Then you can raise the pitch of the first string a little too high, and lower it back down into tune. Again, aim to eliminate the beating. You can then do the same thing, tuning the 6th string, with the 1st.

This double octave is not an interval that you would want to compromise. So it's important to always ensure that it is in good tune.

There are a set of 6 important single octaves on the first three frets, involving an open string, that are in common usage in the home keys. There are a further 2, on the 1st and 3rd frets.

Fine guitar tuning means that all 8 octaves can be relied on to sound good. These are (the "O" showing the open string and the "X" the finger stopping position):

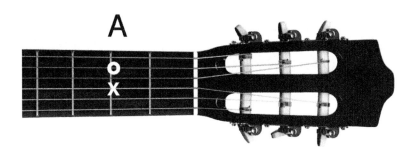

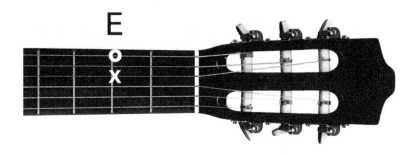

F

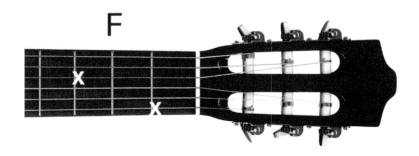

G

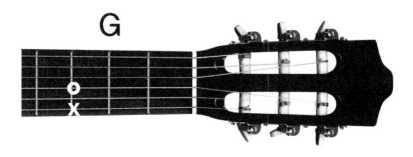

B

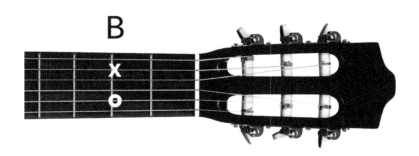

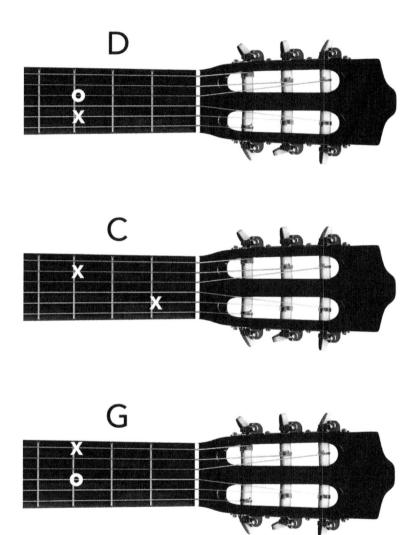

We'll be using these octaves in tuning, a little later. You can use any of them to check the overall tuning of the guitar, at any time. But it is open string intervals that are technically *tuning* intervals, whilst octaves requiring stopped strings, are *check* intervals.

Tuning Intervals Versus *Check* Intervals

Tuning accurately does require listening to beating, so we will be listening to beats. How fast or slow beating is, in an interval that we are tuning, is what we refer to as the *beat rate*. We can only adjust beat rates *smoothly*, on open strings.

So in practice, what we need to do as far as possible, is to alter string tensions whilst listening to open strings, and then *check* other intervals that require stopped strings.

It's not that check intervals are less important. Rather, if a check interval (an interval that requires a stopped note) is the one you need to tune, you can only tune it by tuning open strings, and then checking it. You cannot turn a machine head and stop a note with your left hand, at the same time.

So to sum up, for the tuning to work well, we need to pay a lot of attention to octaves, perfect fifths, perfect fourths, and major thirds. But we will also be paying attention to a major sixth, for practical reasons.

As we tune there are two classes of musical interval that we deal with. The first is intervals between open strings. These can be tuned continuously with the left-hand on the machine head, and are therefore called *tuning intervals*.

The second class is intervals that require stopped strings, where the left-hand has to be on the string in order to hear the interval. These intervals are *check* intervals. However, these are often the most important ones to get right.

Whenever we alter the tension on the string, we should be in control what is happening. So we should never be tuning a string without listening to a *tuning interval,* unless we are very confident about what we're doing. With more experience, and a keen ear, then it's okay to tune check intervals on their own. Unless we are doing *tuning by harmonics,* then we should never be altering *tuning intervals,* without frequently checking the necessary *check* intervals.

The constant alternating between listening to *tuning intervals* and listening to *check intervals* in an efficient manner, *guided by an understanding of what is happening,* is the hallmark of good tuning technique.

Temperament

Let's now take a look at the principles of *temperament*. This is all about the *great circle of fifths*, that we come across in music theory books.

Here is the circle:

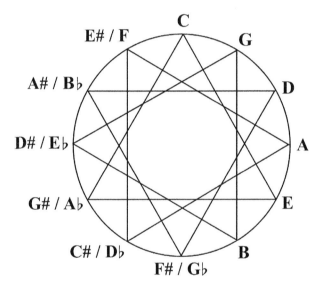

Here, there are some extra straight lines drawn in between the notes. You'll notice that they correspond to what on a keyboard or guitar would be major thirds.

A *temperament* is the precise way in which all the musical intervals round circle, and across the straight lines in the circle, are tuned. We need to dig a little deeper to see why this is an issue to begin with.

Do you remember the series of harmonics that are the ingredients of the tone of a guitar note? Here they are again for the A string and the D string:

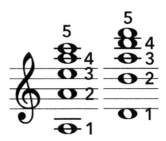

The first five harmonics of the open A string, together with the first five harmonics of the open D string

Each harmonic is a particular sound frequency. Now as it happens, the frequency of each harmonic, for any string, is very close to being a whole number multiple of the frequency of the first harmonic (often called the *fundamental*) of the string.

In the picture above, each number is the *harmonic number* for that string. But because of this principle of the frequencies, it's also indicative of the frequency of that harmonic.

If you multiply the frequency of the *first* harmonic by the number, you'll get the frequency of the higher harmonic. So, for example, for each string, the frequency of harmonic number 3, is 3 times that of harmonic number one.

We already saw that the 4th harmonic of the A string coincides the 3rd harmonic of the D string. So if these two strings are tuned such that the 4th harmonic of the A string is a perfect match with the 3rd harmonic of the D string, then the *fundamental* (1st harmonic) of the D-string will have a frequency 4/3 times the *fundamental* of the A-string.

So when we tune musical intervals *pure* or without beating, there is generally some ratio like this, between the fundamentals of the two notes. For a *pure* perfect fifth, which is beatless, it is 3:2. For an in-tune octave, the ratio is 2:1. And for a *pure* major third, it's 5:4.

So it *is* all about numbers, but for practical tuning we don't need to be too concerned with that. What we are concerned with, is the fact that there will be a particular ratio - in other words, *a particular size* - for each musical interval, in order for that musical interval to be tuned *pure*, or not beating.

But of course no musical interval exists in isolation, on a musical instrument like the guitar or keyboard. All the musical intervals together, that are available on the instrument, have to fit together in one network.

Now let's go back to that *great circle of fifths*. Because the great circle of fifths is a diagram of this network.

Starting at the 12 o'clock position, and *going round clockwise*, we pass through 4 perfect fifths, C to G, G to D, D to A, and A to E. Here's the circle again, to check this out:

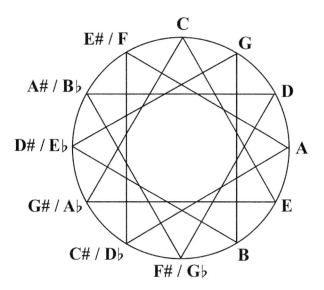

In the clockwise great circle of fifths, the tuning of every major third shown by a straight line, is determined by the tuning of the 4 perfect fifths shown in the short arc of the circumference over the major third line.

We can see from the circle that there is some kind of *relationship* between these four perfect fifths, and the major third along the straight line, C to E.

The 4 segments of the arc, or part of the circumference, *arching over* the straight line, represents the four perfect fifths.

We *could* represent this relationship on a keyboard like this:

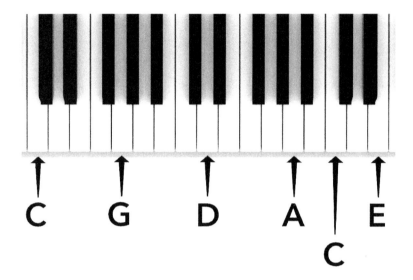

Left to right are the rising perfect fifths C, G, D, A, E. Given that we cannot compromise on the tuning of the octaves here, then the C on the right will be exactly 2 octave above the C on the left. This means that the tuning of these 4 perfect fifths actually *determines* the resultant tuning of the major third C to E.

This is essentially what the great circle of fifths above, is telling us. It's telling us that as long as octaves are in tune, then the tuning of each major third is always determined the tuning of a set of 4 perfect fifths. The circle shows us which perfect fifths determine which major thirds.

But what actually happens is that if we were to tune each one of these 4 perfect fifths *pure*, and beatless (with that ratio 3:2), then the resultant major third C to E *would not be pure*, and beatless (with that ratio 5:4). If we *wanted it* to be pure and beatless then it turns out that we would *have* to have the perfect fifths *beating*.

The way the situation works out, is that the musical distance or size of the interval between the lower and upper notes of each perfect fifth, when they are tuned pure and beatless, makes the interval between the C and E on the right, too *large*. The E ends up too sharp for that major third to be pure and beatless.

The discrepancy between the size of a major third as determined by its associated 4 pure, perfect fifths, and the size of a pure (beatless) major third, is a small interval called the *syntonic comma*. Because the guitar has two of its open strings (G and B) tuned to a major third, the syntonic comma becomes very important in its open string tuning.

Equal Temperament reduces the size of each perfect fifth a little, so that the 4 perfect fifths absorb about 1/3 of the comma, leaving the major third only 2/3 comma wide. So on the equally tempered guitar, the open major third G - B is wide by about 2/3 comma or 8 beats per second.

But because the perfect fifths are narrowed, the perfect fourths are widened, in order to maintain the octaves, because every octave is a perfect fifth plus a perfect fourth. In any octave, and narrowing of the fifth is made up for, by the widening of the fourth. So the open string perfect fourths are tempered wide a little, and should be left slowly beating when correctly tuned.

So every major third is directly connected to 4 perfect fifths. The tuning of these perfect fifths will affect the tuning of the major third, and *vice versa*. In fact, *all* musical notes interconnect and link together in a network that the circle of fifths represents.

It is a network of musical intervals, in which you cannot adjust the tuning of any interval without affecting the tuning of others.

When we understand the great circle of fifths in this way, it is a *temperaments circle*, or *tuning circle*. It's a useful device for showing the generic relationships between the tuning of musical intervals, without necessarily having to refer to where the notes are, in the actual musical compass.

For example, going clockwise round the circumference can represent rising perfect fifths. But it can also represent falling perfect fourths. Or alternatively, going clockwise round the circle could represent going up a perfect fifth to G, and then down the perfect fourth to D, and so on.

The exact way in which all those intervals around the circumference of the circle, are tuned, will determine the resulting tuning in any other interval represented by a straight line in the circle. The network of all the possible musical intervals (excluding double accidentals) looks like this:

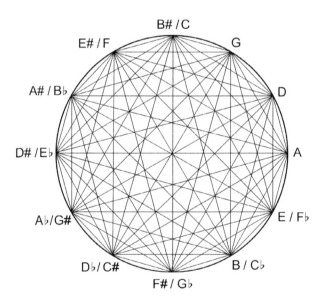

As you can see, it's quite a complex network. The precise arrangement of the tuning in all the intervals is called a *temperament*. When intervals are slightly mistuned away from being tuned pure, or beatless, they are said to be *tempered*.

In the circle, it is impossible for most of the intervals not to be "mistuned" away from their pure or beatless state, in some way. A *temperament* is a specific way of controlling this, by choosing which intervals to temper, and by how much.

The standard, modern temperament in use today, is called *Equal Temperament*. This is the temperament in the design of the guitar, that determines the positions of the frets.

You'll notice in the circle above that there are lines connecting notes that are a semitone apart, such as, for example, B# / C to Db / C#. Even the sizes of the semitones are determined by the chosen tuning in other intervals, or in other words, by the temperament.

It is all an interconnected network of all the musical intervals, in which theoretically, no interval can be altered in isolation, without affecting other intervals.

In Equal Temperament all the semitones are the same musical size. (Remember that the reason the frets on the guitar are not all an equal distance apart, is because that's how the fret separation distances works out when all the semitones are the same size, *as a musical interval*. On the fingerboard arrangement, it's all about *ratios* rather than absolute distances).

Wide and Narrow

Equal sized semitones are achieved by tuning all the perfect fifths a little *smaller* than a pure or beatless perfect fifth. This means that the upper note of a perfect fifth, if tuned against the lower note, is tuned a little flatter than beatless.

Alternatively, the lower note is likewise tuned a little sharp from its beatless tuning position.

This is often described as tuning the perfect fifth a little *narrow*. In other words, you can expect there to be a very small amount of beating (a slow beat) due to the "musical distance" between the two notes of the perfect fifths, being *narrower* than pure - the two notes are musically closer together.

In Equal Temperament other intervals such as major thirds, and perfect fourths, are *wider* than pure. This means that the two notes of the interval are further apart than they would be if the interval were beatless.

When any interval is tuned narrow it will beat. Likewise, it will beat if it is tuned wide. Only when it is "pure", in which case it is neither wide nor narrow, will it be beatless.

As it turns out, in Equal Temperament, the *only* intervals that are theoretically pure or beatless are the octaves (and multiple octaves) and unisons. Every single other interval is *tempered*, either wide, or narrow.

So in Equal Temperament, whenever we encounter any musical interval other than an octave or a unison, we can *expect* it to be beating either wide or narrow, depending on the interval. But that doesn't mean that unpleasantly beating intervals can be excused under the label of *Equal Temperament*.

In Equal Temperament the amount of deviation (tempering) from pure tuning is *very precise*. At least, it is, in theory. And one of the characteristics of Equal Temperament is that the amount of tempering in the perfect fifths and fourths is sufficiently small that in general playing, you hardly notice it. However, on the guitar, it's often made worse (faster beating), because of *stopping sharp* and *false beating* etc.

It is the thirds (and tenths) and sixths that in Equal Temperament are most deviated from being *pure* (beatless). That's why, in tuning the guitar, without precision, it is easy to end up with unpleasantly intoned, course sounding thirds and sixths.

If we try to tune the perfect fourths and perfect fifths all pure, most of the thirds and sixth just get worse, as a consequence of the temperament circle. They end up far faster beating than they are meant to be, in Equal Temperament.

So for practical tuning purposes the first thing we need to know or remember about Equal Temperament, is which intervals are *intended to be* narrow, and which ones are *intended to be* wide.

The ones we'll be tuning in practice, are:

- Perfect fifth - NARROW by a small amount
- Perfect twelfth (perfect fifth plus an octave) - NARROW by a small amount
- Perfect fourth - WIDE by a small amount
- Major third - considerably WIDE
- Major sixth - considerably WIDE
- Major tenth (octave plus a major third) - considerably WIDE

In practice, if we pay attention to these, the other tempered intervals we haven't mentioned will generally take care of themselves.

Fast And Slow

So tempered intervals fall all into two kinds: *fast beating* and *slow beating*.

The tempered perfect intervals - perfect fourths and perfect fifths (and perfect twelfths) - are *slow beating* tempered intervals, that realistically on the guitar are around one or two beats per second in the middle of the compass.

All the other tempered intervals - notably the major thirds and major sixths - are *fast beating*. This is one reason why the open major third between the 2nd and 3rd strings, often seems to be the centre of tuning problems. It is the only open string pair with a fast beat rate - theoretically around 8 beats per second. The other adjacent string pairs are tuned to perfect fourths, and are therefore slow beating.

The fast beating intervals are intervals that we can accept much faster beating in, than we can in the slow beating intervals. For example, the 8 beats per second in the open string major third G - B, is acceptable. If you put 8 beats per second in one of the open string pairs that is a perfect fourth (which is supposed to be a slow beating interval), say, A - D, it sounds dreadful.

What often makes major thirds and sixths on the guitar turn out too wide, is the way *false beating* affects the tuning of the *slow beating* intervals. Remember that false beating is *slow beating* that occurs in single strings, rather than two strings that make a tempered or mistuned interval (it happens because the string is free to vibrate in more than one transverse plane).

Even if we know about Equal Temperament and temper our perfect fourths and fifths, we can still end up with the thirds too wide, and beating too fast. This is because there is the tendency to tune the fourths and fifths too pure, in trying to overcome false beating.

If a string has false beating, what may sound to us like a tempered interval, may well be an interval tuned pure, except that it has the false beating in it. The effect this has on the major thirds, is to make them wider, and beating faster.

In the fast beating intervals, the thirds and sixths, false beating tends to be more noticeable as increasing and decreasing in the beat rate of the interval.

It is simply not possible to successfully tune a guitar with the major third on the open strings G - B tuned beatless. *Ad hoc* tuning often results either in this interval having a much faster beat rate than 8 per second, which makes it unpleasantly course, or, if it is deliberately slowed down, it results in over-tempered fourths and fifths, which sound unpleasant.

Try listening to the beating between the 2nd and 3rd strings now. If the guitar is tuned simply by stopping adjacent strings on the 5th frets, or 4th fret in the case of the G string, as we outlined at the beginning of the book, then you will find there is quite a fast beat rate between the open G and B strings.

To hear it clearly, the trick is to *listen at the right pitch*. The pitch of the beating harmonic is two octaves above the pitch of the B string. You can find the pitch of it by playing the harmonic on the B string. Touch lightly on the B string over the 5th fret, pluck the string, and remember that pitch. Keep your ear focused on that pitch, as you pluck the open 2nd and 3rd strings. You should hear the beating very clearly.

For practical tuning purposes we do need to remember that in Equal Temperament all the major thirds and major tenths are *considerably wider than pure*, whilst perfect fourths are just a little wide, and perfect fifths a little narrow.

For intervals around the part of the fingerboard up to the third fret, major thirds have beat rates on the bass strings of a few beats per second, ranging up to 10 or more beats per second on the treble strings.

In contrast, on a well tuned guitar, the open perfect fourths have only around one beat per second or less, and the perfect fifths less than that. Unfortunately, *stopping sharp will* make these beat rates faster.

We *must* always bear this principle in mind, that major thirds (and major sixths) are quite fast beating wide, whilst perfect fourths are slow beating wide, and perfect fifths are slow beating narrow. We must bear this in mind whatever set of notes we are tuning. If we do, it will make understanding what is going on, *much* easier.

Having said all this, it turns out, in practice, that whilst the business of temperament forms the backdrop or main canvas on which we're working when tuning the guitar, it is by no means the end of the story. As far as guitar tuning is concerned, there are some things that are just as big an influence on what we need to do when tuning, as the temperament itself. And that's what we'll look at, next.

Stopping Sharp

We've seen that the basic tuning configuration of the guitar is Equal Temperament. This means that we can expect the major thirds to be beating wide, the perfect fourths to be slowly beating wide, and the perfect fifths to be beating slowly, narrow.

It is excessive beating in intervals that contributes most to them sounding poorly tuned. On a keyboard or well-tuned piano some beating *is* present, but highly organised, and with only gradual changes in beat rate across the compass. Most people are unaware of it on keyboards and pianos, but whether or not we are consciously aware of it, it is an expected and intended part of the sound.

The tuning of the guitar is generally a lot less stable than that of the keyboard. As equally tempered instruments fall out of tune, what tends to happen is that the beat rates in the thirds (and sixths), perfect fourths, and perfect fifths, change in such a way that whilst some beat rates may decrease, making the intervals sweeter-sounding, the majority increase, making the intervals sound worse.

This is a predictable effect of the principles temperament, and of the network of intervals. At the same time, the octaves fall out of tune, and start beating, which is always detrimental.

When perfect fourths or perfect fifths on the guitar beat too fast, the intervals begin to sound sour. However, a small amount of beating is natural to the tone of guitar strings anyway, and is accommodated well in the sound of the instrument. Well tuned perfect fourths and perfect fifths, in

Equal Temperament, are slow-beating anyway (around one or two beats per second, or less).

When it comes to major thirds or major tenths, then we are in a different ballpark. The *theoretical beat rate* for the open 2nd and 3rd strings, B and G, in Equal Temperament, is about 8 beats per second. Compared to the perfect fourths and perfect fifths, that's very fast. The interval is already a long way detuned from its pure, beatless state, in which it has the sweetest tone.

On the piano, these fast beat rates in major thirds and tenths are often said to contribute to the tone of the instrument in a positive way, making its tone "shimmer". However, the guitar is a very different instrument, and many guitarists will be aware of how much sweeter the major thirds and tenths sound, if they don't beat.

In any case, if the guitar is not in good tune, and a major third or tenth has become too wide, then the whole intonation and tone of the interval really does sound too course.

So what we are trying to achieve when tuning the guitar is the avoidance of excessive beating in the intervals. We can never get rid of all of it, everywhere, because of the principle of temperament. But what we can do, is take control of it, in a way that avoids unpleasant surprises or consequences.

The principle of Equal Temperament is that the intonation is the same in all keys. Anyone who has tried to tune a guitar, either using the 5th and 4th frets method, or using an electronic meter, is likely to have found that often, the result is not intonation that is the same and all keys. This is not generally a result of some error in the guitar, such as in the fret positions. Rather, it is hidden in deeper issues that we have been talking about.

Although the guitar is designed for Equal Temperament, most guitarists probably don't spend most of their time playing literally in all keys, in one session. So it often actually makes sense for many guitarists to deviate from Equal Temperament a small amount, in a way that favours the sweetness of tuning in the keys in use, at the expense of keys not being played in.

This is something that always used to be done on keyboard instruments in the days before Equal Temperament was adopted for the piano. To do it effectively, is simply a matter of understanding the principles of temperament, and applying them as we wish. On the guitar, however, the matter is complicated by the fixed fret positions.

The basic theory of temperament works out what beat rates to expect where, but it is based on some ideal assumptions that don't always reflect the actual situation with real guitar strings. This brings us back to what we mentioned earlier, which is that the "harmonics" we are listening to when we are listening to beating, are not really true harmonics.

In practice, guitar strings are made from materials that have stiffness as well as the flexibility necessary to work as a musical string. This stiffness, even in a perfectly good string, introduces the *inharmonicity*. This is why sound engineers and scientists will often say that it is not really harmonics we're listening to, but *inharmonic partials*.

We don't really need to get into the theory of this, but in general it means these sound ingredients we are listening to, that are producing the beating we can hear, tend to be a little sharper or higher in pitch than they would otherwise be, if they had been true harmonics.

Not only can this sometimes change the beat rates from what temperament theory says they should be, but it can also cause a change to the apparent musical pitch of a string. This is because our ear and brain unconsciously assesses musical pitch on the basis of how the harmonics or partials are distributed.

Sound engineers and scientists sometimes call the effects of string stiffness, or inharmonicity, *dispersion*, meaning that the partials become more *dispersed* or separated.

This is why stopped strings, particularly as they age, *stop sharp*. The musical pitch of the stopped string can sound unexpectedly high, even if by only a very small amount, and the beat rates in intervals that include the stopped note, are affected.

Strings can also *stop flat*. New strings can typically stop flat, and old strings, if they become worn at the fret position, or have other damage, can stop flat. However, stopping sharp is the most common condition, and although it may not be noticed as such, it will affect subsequent beat rates and the tuning condition of intervals that include stopped notes.

Stopping sharp generally becomes more acute the higher up the fingerboard you are stopping. Sometimes this may also be due to the extra distance the string has to be pushed down, to reach the fret, which increases string tension. But really, that should already be taken into account in the positioning of the frets.

The main reason it typically becomes more acute higher up the fingerboard is because the speaking length of the string is made shorter. Inharmonicity increases *exponentially* as the speaking length of the string becomes shorter.

Stopping sharp can also be acute close to the nut, i.e. on the first fret. If you find persistent tuning issues lower down the fingerboard, *i.e.* closer to the nut, you're not likely to be able to solve them by adopting tuning methods based on high stopping positions.

Similarly, tuning by matching partials over the 5th and 7th frets will fail to address stopping-sharp problems if they are present. And tuning by unisons between strings stopped on the 5th or 4th fret, and adjacent open strings, which gives a basic tuning, will be compromised if strings are stopping sharp on those frets.

Unlike a keyboard, the guitar is a stringed instrument that relies on manual adjustment of the speaking lengths of the strings, by stopping on the frets. This, in itself, is not a clear-cut "black and white" matter.

It is perfectly normal on many guitars, to be able to change the tension and tuning of a string a little, simply by altering how hard you press with your finger behind the fret. When playing chords, it's perfectly possible for one or more fingers to not be positioned optimally behind the fret, which will affect the tuning. Correcting that, is not a tuning problem, but a matter of technique. So there is actually some considerable opportunity of tuning on-the-fly, as we play.

Nevertheless, everyone wants a good foundation to work on. And that means having to deal both with the principles of temperament, and the principles of stopping sharp (or even flat), in tuning the instrument to begin with.

Some guitarists, in attempting to correct tuning problems, end up with hugely compromised octaves. In all temperaments octaves are supposed to be sacrosanct, and untempered. There nothing quite like an out-of-tune octave for wrecking intonation.

However, on the guitar there is a limit to how sacrosanct they can be. And that's not because of our own tuning inability in any way. It's because there are considerations other than temperament, like *stopping sharp*, imposing on the whole tuning situation. We often have to allow a *little* compromise on octaves.

Remember that the vibratory motion of any guitar string is in general, actually *elliptical*. This means that even a single harmonic can *beat*, because it acts like two different harmonics at two slightly different pitches; one in one plane of motion, and the other in another plane of motion.

If you're trying to leave a small amount of beating in an interval, it may be the *false beat* that you are listening to, rather than the result of you actually tempering the interval. And if you do temper an interval, you may well have to have more or faster beating in it, than theoretically, you would expect.

Even a well-tuned octave on a guitar generally has *some* beating present in it, somewhere, in some harmonic. It's all a question of degree. When we say we tune an octave beatless, it's *qualitative*, rather than genuinely *quantitative*.

In the end, the tuning you achieve, depends on the guitar, the strings, and your own artistic judgements. However, that doesn't mean that you can get really good tuning by artistic judgements alone. Because behind any tuning, are hard structural rules, that come from the business of temperament, and stopping sharp.

Practical Points to Remember

We said that *tuning intervals* are intervals that can be *tuned continuously*, turning the machine head. Essentially, they are intervals between open strings. Check intervals are literally intervals that are *checked in-between* turns to the machine head.

Check intervals are often more important than *tuning intervals*. They are not merely something you check, to make sure your tuning interval is right. Often, the check interval is *the one you most want to get right.*

If you are familiar with guitar tuning then you don't *necessarily* have to use tuning intervals at all. It is possible to adjust the tuning of the string a micro-amount, just by listening to the change in pitch, or even by turning the machine head without listening to anything. So it is possible to tune a check interval in a series of separate turns of the machine head.

Often though, you'll want to change the tuning of a *check interval,* and hear the precise amount by which you are altering the string, by listening to it beating against another string. This is how you get fine, continuous control. You have to do this using a *tuning interval* between open strings, which leaves your left hand free to turn the machine head.

The octaves are highly important check intervals. They should never be left compromised in an uncontrolled way. The only octaves we can use as *tuning interval*s is the double octave between the first and sixth open strings, the two Es.

We've already said how tuning issues can centre around the 2nd and 3rd strings because they are tuned to a major third, with a relatively fast beat rate. In addition to this, the 2nd and 3rd strings can be prone to inharmonicity and stopping-sharp issues, especially on an old 3rd string of a classical guitar.

Inharmonicity increases exponentially with the string diameter, and is worse, the lower the string tension. On the guitar the 1st string has the highest tension and the smallest diameter, and so is in general the least inharmonic. The strings then become thicker, and lower tension.

However, coil-covered strings are less stiff for their diameter, which reduces their inharmonicity. They are also much more flexible and less prone to inharmonicity if their core is floss rather than solid (as is always the case on a classical guitar).

Remember though, that sometimes, and especially with new strings, strings can actually stop *flat*. Essentially, the tuning method we're going to use can still be used for flat stopping strings, but the intervals will behave differently.

An effective way to deal with the issues that arise from the open major third, and stopping sharp issues around this area, is to tackle this part of the tuning first, head on. The method we are going to use, does this.

Wide Versus Narrow

One thing worth mentioning before we embark on the method, concerns wide or narrow tempered intervals. We've talked about this already, but we need to be very clear on it, as we are tuning, so that's why we are coming back to it.

Think of the interval like a spring. Unstretched, and uncompressed, it is its "pure" size, and tuned beatless. You you can think of each note as being at each end of the spring. If you stretch the spring, you're making the interval wide. If you compress it, you're making it narrow.

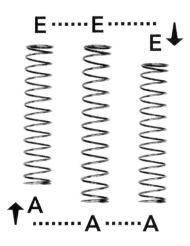

Springs representing the perfect fifth A to E. The spring in the middle is neither compressed nor stretched. It represents the beatless interval. A compressed spring represents a narrow, beating interval. If the pitch of the A is raised, the spring becomes compressed. If the pitch of the E is lowered, the spring also becomes compressed. Either way, the interval beats narrow. The more it is stretched or compressed, the faster it beats.

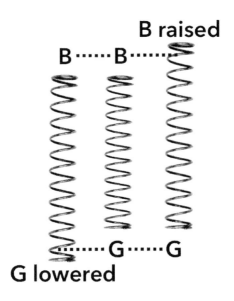

B raised

B ······ B ······

G lowered ······ G ····· G

Springs representing the major third G to B. The spring in the middle is neither compressed nor stretched. It represents the beatless interval. A stretched spring represents a wide, beating interval. If the pitch of the B is raised, the spring becomes stretched. If the pitch of the G is lowered, the spring also becomes stretched. Either way, the interval beats wide. The more it is stretched, the faster it beats.

So if when raising the upper note the beat rate increases, then the interval is wide. If it is already beating and the rate decreases when raising the upper note, then the interval is narrow.

The other way around, if you are lowering the upper note, then a decrease in beat rate means a wide interval, and an increase, means a narrow interval.

Similarly, if the beat rate increases when raising the lower note, then the interval is narrow. And if the rate decreases when raising the lower note, then the interval is wide.

The other way around, if the beat rate increases on lowering the lower note, the interval is wide. And if the rate decreases on lowering the lower note, in the interval is narrow.

In the instructions below we'll say whether an interval is wide or narrow, and what effect raising or lowering the tension of the string will have on the beat rate, *assuming the interval is not "on the wrong side"*.

An interval "on the wrong side" is one that is narrow when it is meant to be wide, or *vice versa*. Generally speaking, in *fine-tuning* the guitar, this won't happen. But in case you ever suspect it *has* happened, bear in mind the following:

The beat rate in an interval gets faster as it gets wider, or as it gets narrower. The beat *rate* by itself cannot tell you whether the interval is wide and narrow. You can only tell that for sure, by actually increasing or decreasing the beat rate, and knowing whether it is the upper or lower note you are adjusting.

Estimating Beat Rates

It's quite easy to estimate the beat rates we'll need, if you are a musician and used to dealing with rhythms. The first thing is to get reliable idea of how long a second of time is. Without using a clock, watch, or stopwatch, there are a number of "trick" words or phrases you can use to give you the length of the second.

One popular one is the word *Mississippi*. If you say "one Mississippi, two Mississippi, three Mississippi", and so on, at a normal, lively conversational speed, that will give you a good idea of counting seconds. Sometimes people use the phrase "*little minute*" instead of *Mississippi*.

You can find your own preferred word or phrase, and test it against the second hand of watch. It doesn't take much practice to learn to do the counting silently, in your head.

Fortunately, for tuning the guitar, it is not necessary to count many different beat rates, accurately. We need to have the perfect fifths or perfect twelfths we are going to tune, beating *less* than 2 per second - about 1.5 at most and preferably less.

Theoretically, they should be *much* slower than this. We will aim to get them as slow as possible, but in practice, on the guitar, stopping sharp and false beating, whilst not at all intrusive, still means that we will be lucky to get the theoretical beat rate.

Theoretically, perfect fourths in the same part of the compass as perfect fifths, should be about twice as fast as the fifths. But in practice, on the guitar, the open perfect fourths are going to sound more or less the same, or even *less tempered*, than the perfect fifths and perfect twelfths.

The fast beating intervals are a different matter. The theoretical beat rate for the open 2nd and 3rd strings, which is a major third, is 8 beats per second. If you can count seconds, this is easy enough to judge.

Musically it's literally a fast 8 beats in a bar, counting one bar each second. Or, you can work up to it, so to speak, by first dividing your seconds rhythm into 2, then doubling the speed of the rhythm to 4, then 8.

Similarly, for a beat rate of six beats per second, which is the beat rate of the major sixth between the open 4th and 2nd strings, just think of a fast 6/8 rhythm (six beats to the bar) for bars at one per second.

With a little practice, basic beat rate values like one per second, two every three seconds (1.5 beats per second), 2 second, 3 per second, 4 per second, 6 per second, and 8 per second, become recognisable and familiar even without counting. All it takes, is some practice.

It's a good idea to practice familiarity with beat rates on the open 2nd and 3rd strings major third, by altering the B string, and listening to, and counting the beats. The sound of eight 8 per second in that interval should become familiar. You should also develop a keen ear for when this beat rate is faster than 8 per second, which is to be avoided.

It's a good idea to keep the string grooves across the nut lubricated with a suitable lubricant (graphite is sometimes used, but today a polymer lubricant may be used). Otherwise, the string can stick at this point due to friction, making smooth tuning more difficult.

Finally, in estimating beat rates we always should bear in mind three influences that can make what we are listening to misleading, and possibly cause wrong decisions.

The first of these is the false beats that we have already spoken of. False beats, remember, are slow beats that are already present in the sound of single strings. We'll experience the effects of these most in the slow beating intervals - the perfect fourths and fifths. The effect they have will invariably be to *increase* the apparent beat rate in the interval, and/or make it impossible to have the interval genuinely beatless.

The second is *variable beat rates*. These are caused by false beating, and happen when the beat rate in a fast beating interval - such as major thirds and tenths - has a beat rate that changes as it proceeds, even though the string tensions remain the same. Often, this means the beat rate will *cycle* between a minimum and a maximum. The beat rate we hear immediately after plucking the string, will be different to what we hear a couple of seconds later.

The third is that the main beating harmonic in an interval, will have another beating harmonic at a pitch an octave above, and this secondary harmonic will have about twice the beat rate. The beat rates quoted throughout this book are for the first, or lower harmonic. If we mistake the higher harmonic for the first, we will assess the tempering of the interval as being much more than it actually is.

When we come to the tuning method, there will be instructions on where (at which pitch) to listen.

On Random Adjustments

When an interval sounds out of tune, there is always the temptation to pick on the apparently offending string, and adjust the offending interval by tuning that string.

This can work, sometimes, but is also at risk of leading into a random, *ad hoc* tuning situation, which just gets worse and worse. The principles of temperament alone, will always work against us unless we take deliberate command of them.

Any interval that sounds out of tune has *two* notes. It may be one, or the other, or *both* notes that have moved. You cannot tell which it is, without further checks. And you can't simply check whether other connected intervals are out of tune. It is necessary to appreciate whether intervals are *wide* or *narrow*.

When we are very familiar with the principles temperament, and how it is affected by the effects of stopping sharp, then it is possible to make random adjustments. But you have to have a good instant grasp of which intervals you are expecting to be wide, which ones you are expecting to be narrow, and how they fit together.

So actually, by far the easiest way to deal with a situation in which a single string appears to have gone out of tune, is to quickly run through the entire tuning sequence, in the form of just testing various intervals *in their tuning sequence*. It doesn't take long, because there are, after all, only six strings.

Running through the sequence, listening to the intervals, is the quickest way to ascertain where the problem really lies, and what you need to do about it.

The following tuning method is a *tuning sequence*. It requires tuning the strings in a specific order. Once you have trained your ear to hear the beats, and once you are familiar with the sequence, and the checks, it is as fast as any other method.

However, explaining it in detail is quite long-winded. Don't be put off by this. It's far less of an effort than actually learning to play the guitar!

Tuning Methods

Equal Temperament Tuning

Preliminary Outline

This chapter goes into great detail. But despite the length of the chapter, once learned, the method is suitable for speed tuning.

The trick behind this tuning method is in the use of fast beating intervals as the backbone of the tuning.

The fast beating intervals are the most reliable stepping stones through the tuning sequence. We are going to make sure that the fast beating intervals have about the right beat rate, but at the same time adjust the slow beating intervals, around them.

It's very easy to make mistakes with slow beating intervals, because they can be very wayward in the way they behave, and their beat rates are very affected by false beating and stopping sharp. It's quite easy to think you have the right result, when you haven't.

The fast beating intervals are like signposts to good compromises in the slow beating intervals. So we can to some extent overcome any effects of false beating and stopping sharp, in the perfect fifths and fourths, by relying on the fast beating intervals. As long as you can count 4, 6 and 8 beats in a second, then you can do this tuning method easily.

It may take a little practice to learn to hear beating in the intervals, but the instructions are all here, and it's well worth it. This is a fine-tuning technique - it isn't something you can learn from scratch in just five minutes, but once learned, the method itself is quick and reliable. Like learning to play the guitar, regular practise pays off in the end.

What we're doing is applying the best rendering of Equal Temperament to the guitar, in a way that takes account of all those factors that affect guitar tuning, that in themselves, have nothing to do temperament.

In the traditional theory of temperament the pure tuning of octaves is sacrosanct. The octaves are not tempered. However, the actual physical factors in many musical instruments means that in practice octaves are often not truly pure octaves. Even in piano tuning expert tuners often "stretch" octaves in a judicious way, in order to take account of the effects of inharmonicity, due to stiffness in the strings.

In tuning the guitar the effects of strings stopping sharp often means that certain octaves have to be compromised very slightly if we are to avoid other intervals, involving the notes of the octave, becoming unacceptably tempered.

The method given here is not the only possibility. But it has been rationally worked out to give an efficient result, once you're familiar with judging beat rates between 4 and 8 per second, and have a good idea of what you find acceptable as a slow beat rate in your perfect fifths and fourths.

You may want to work out your own variant tuning method along the same lines.

1: The 4th string (D)

The 4th string, D, can be easily tuned from a standard A 440 Hz tuning fork (or electronic tone, or other reference source). The audible pitch and frequency of the fork coincides with the 3rd harmonic (partial) of the D string. You can play this harmonic and familiarise yourself with its musical pitch, by touching the string lightly over the 7th fret, and plucking the string.

When you hear the harmonic, that's the pitch to listen for. However, in actually tuning, just listen to the open string. The harmonic is still there, whether beating or not, in the sound of the open string. We can tune the string beatless to the fork.

(If you can't be sure that your tuning is beatless, perhaps because of false beats, then there is a strategy to follow. It is better to err slightly on the side of beating sharp, rather than flat, because the third harmonic of the string is likely to be slightly sharp, rather than flat, due to inharmonicity).

Having tuned the D string to the fork or other reference source, this becomes our tuning *datum point*. We don't want to go changing it again, unless it is by tuning it again to the fork (or whatever pitch reference you are using).

2: The 2nd string (B)

Tuning Interval: **D - B Major Sixth**

(harmonic pitch 2nd string, 7th fret)

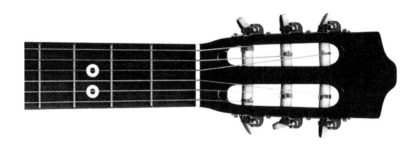

Check Interval: **D - D Octave**

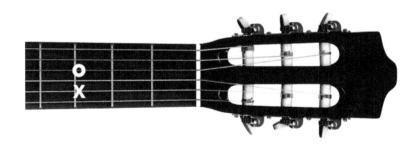

Check Interval: **E - B Perfect Fifth**

(harmonic pitch 2nd string, 12th fret)

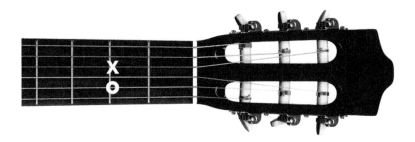

We now need to tune the 2nd string in a way that accommodates any inharmonicity and stopping sharp that may be occurring on this string. It requires listening to the tempering of the fast beating open major sixth D to B, between the 4th and 2nd strings.

You can find the pitch of the harmonic that you should be listening to, in the tuning of this interval, by touching the 2nd string over the 7th fret. Fix your attention on this pitch, and when playing the open sixth, and you will hear it beating at that pitch.

Major sixths in Equal Temperament beat wide. This means that when you lower the tension in the 2nd string, the beat rate will *reduce*. If you raise the 2nd string, the beat rate will *increase*.

If you have lubricated the string grooves across the nut then it should be possible to make fine changes to the beat rate. (If there is still sticking, then it is possible to *gently* apply finger pressure to the string just beyond the nut to overcome any sticking when raising the tension. When lowering the tension sticking can be overcome by pulling upwards on the string in its speaking length).

The *theoretical* beat rate for the open D to B sixth is about 6.5 beats per second. You don't really want the beat rate to be faster than this. If you end up with it sounding a little slower, at around 6 per second, that's fine.

We should not compromise the octave D (open) to D (2nd string, 3rd fret), other than by the very tiniest amount. You may well find, due to the 2nd string stopping sharp on the 3rd fret, that with the best octave D - D you can have the open major sixth beating more slowly than 6 beats per second. This is fine, but we should not have more than the theoretical 6.5 beats in this major sixth.

However, you can't *only* adjust the open major sixth D to B to suit the octave D - D. We also have to consider the perfect fifth E (4th string, 2nd fret) to B (open). The octave will want to B string to be as low as possible, whilst the perfect fifth will want the B to be as high as possible.

Method

Remember that when checking stopped intervals the tension on the string will be increased with increasing finger pressure behind the fret (especially on a steel-strung guitar). If an octave is good, it should sound good easily, without having to use excessive finger pressure, or excessively little finger pressure.

Open sixth and octave

Listen to the beat rate in the open sixth D - B. Does it sound faster or slower than 6 beats per second, or about equal to 6 beats? Check the octave D - D. If it is not beating, even slightly, and the sixth D - B has around six or less beats per second, then you can go on to check the perfect fifth (see below).

Otherwise, lower the tension of the B string to make the beat rate in the sixth D - B deliberately too slow. (If you go too far and the sixth is beating narrow, or *on the wrong side*, you can also raise the tension checking the B against the D string stopped on the 9th fret - which gives the same note. This helps if you are not sure about what is going on).

Now check the octave D - D. If it has worsened, this is good. If it has not worsened, then go back to the major sixth and lower the second string some more, until the octave worsens. This is necessary to make sure that the octave is narrow and not wide. Also, for mechanical reasons we want to bring the second string into tune on a tension raise, and not by lowering its tension.

Once you know the octave is definitely narrow, go back to the major sixth and raise the second string little, increasing its beat rate, but keeping it no more than 6 per second. How gradually you do this is up to you. Each time, re-check the octave. Gradually bring the second string up, listening to the major sixth, until the octave check is good.

Perfect fifth

Now check the perfect fifth E (4th string 2nd fret) to B (open 2nd string). This interval will be *narrow*. To hear the *pitch* of the harmonic to listen to, lightly touch the 2nd string of the 12th fret. Listen out for beating *at this pitch* when playing the perfect fifth.

Because the perfect fifth is narrow, lowering the second string will *increase* the beat rate. Raising the second string tension will *decrease* its beat rate.

If you already have a successful D - D octave then the question is "is this perfect fifth acceptable"? It *should* beat, but if it is beating faster than you can accept, then you will have to *raise* the B string. It should be no more than about 2 beats per second. Slower than that is fine. Its theoretical rate is about one beat every two seconds, but unless you have no inharmonicity and stopping sharp, then you are unlikely to achieve this.

If you do have to raise the B string, then go back to the major sixth and increase its beat rate very slightly. Check the octave D - D to see if it is still acceptable, and then check the perfect fifth E - B again.

You are aiming to get the best compromise between these three intervals. There is some, but *very little*, flexibility in what is an acceptable octave tuning. There is a little more flexibility in the tuning of the perfect fifth. There is most flexibility in the tuning of the major sixth, but we *are* aiming to have its beat rate no faster than 6.5 per second. This is an important principle that will pay off in its effects later.

If you have a good octave, and the perfect fifth is acceptable, but you haven't got a slower than 6 per second beat rate in the open sixth E - B, then so be it. But remember there is some flexibility in the tuning of the octave. So if the octave sounds good, but the open sixth is beating too fast, try lowering the second string and tuning up again.

The octave will have a tendency to be too wide (the D on the third fret of the 2nd string too *sharp*), whilst the perfect fifth will have a tendency to be too narrow (the

2nd string too *flat*). You have to find the right compromise between the two.

Raising the tension of the 2nd string will make the major sixth more tempered, but will make the perfect fifth less tempered. The aim is to get a desirable balance between these two, without compromising the octave too much.

If there is no stopping sharp on the strings then tuning the B string is all about the octave being good, and the right amount temperament in a perfect fifth and the major sixth.

If the strings are stopping sharp, then the tuning is effectively all about how sharp the B string stops on the 3rd fret, and how sharp the D string stops on the second fret.

3: The 3rd string (G)

Tuning Interval: **G - B Major Third**
(harmonic pitch 2nd string, 5th fret)

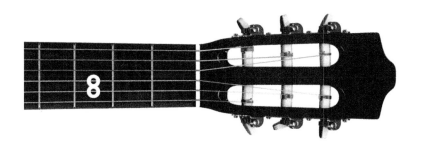

Tuning Interval: D - G Perfect Fourth
(harmonic pitch 3rd string, 7th fret)

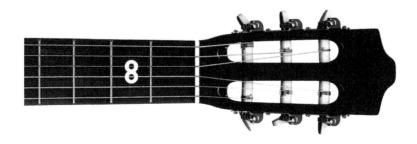

Primary *Check Interval*: G - C Perfect Fourth
(harmonic pitch 3rd string, 5th fret)

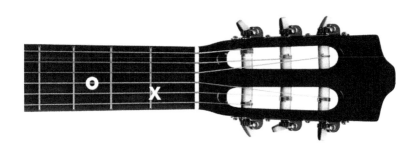

Primary *Check Interval*: G - D Perfect Fifth
(harmonic pitch 3rd string, 7th fret)

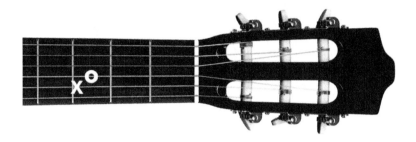

Secondary *Check Interval*: D - A Perfect Fifth
(harmonic pitch 4th string, 7th fret)

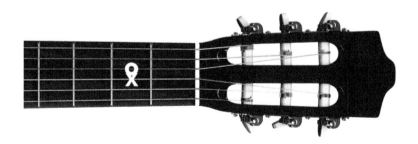

Method

What we're doing in tuning the G string is taking care of both the temperament, and any stopping sharp that is occurring on the B string (which affects the fifth and the fourth that we are checking).

The checking cycle

We are going to tune up the 3rd string, listening to the open major third G - B, until the beat rate is a little faster than the open major sixth D - B, at almost 8 per second. But it may end up a little closer to the open major sixth.

We tune the open G - B and each time we detect a change in the G - B third tuning interval, we need to compare it to the sixth D - B, and also *check the two primary check intervals*, the G - D fifth and the G - C fourth, both on the 2nd and 3rd strings. We *cycle through this procedure*. If in bringing the G up, we overshoot and bring it too sharp, we lower it again and bring it up again.

We are aiming to get both the fifth and the fourth beat rates about the same, ideally, or the fourth G - C just a little faster than the fifth. Until the G string is in tune, the tendency will be for the fourth to be faster than the fifth.

So as we tune up the G string, we are slowing down the fourth, but speeding up the fifth. The slowdown in the fourth is at the expense of the fifth.

So begin by lowering the 3rd string until the beat rate between the 2nd and 3rd strings is too fast (faster than 8 beats per second). Now if you check the perfect fifth (open 3rd string to 2nd string, 3rd fret) and the perfect fourth (open 3rd string to 2nd string, 1st fret), you should find both are too fast. After tuning up the string, neither should be more than 2 per second, at the most. Don't let the fifth beat faster than the fourth.

The open third G - B must be faster than the sixth D - B, but we really don't want it to have *more* than 8 beats per second. There is no reason due to stopping sharp that this would need to be the case, and in terms of temperament, it is unnecessary. This open third sounds sweeter, the slower its beat rate.

Remember that as we tune up the G string the two primary checks, the perfect fourth G - C and the perfect fifth G - D *work as a pair*. Once we are fine tuning, the fifth gets faster (less desirable) as the fourth gets slower (more desirable), as you raise the G string. Stop where there is a good balance between the two, where the third G - B is a bit faster than the sixth D - B.

Secondary Checks

You can check the open fourth D - G (4th and 3rd strings) and the perfect fifth D - A (open 4th string and 3rd string, 2nd fret). But you should find these are perfectly satisfactory (because of the temperament the fourth will be a little wide, and the fifth a little narrow - both have a *slow* beat).

Problem Solving

If your primary checks of the perfect fifth and perfect fourth on the 2nd and 3rd strings doesn't sound right, then here is the scenario:

If the perfect fourth still beats much faster than the perfect fifth, then raise the G string listening to and decreasing the beat rate in the open G - B, until the fourth slows down.

If you ever find the fifth is beating faster than the fourth, then you will need to re-lower the G string, and tune it back up again.

When the fifth and fourth are about the same, or the fourth just a little faster, the beat rate in the open G - B should be correct. It should be 8 beats per second. If it is not, and yet the other checks seem to work out perfectly, then re-check the octave D (open string) to D (on the B string) to make sure that the B string hasn't moved. If it has, you need to re-tune it, and then re-tune the G string.

4: The 5th string (A)

Tuning Interval: **A - D Perfect Fourth**
(harmonic pitch 4th string, 7th fret)

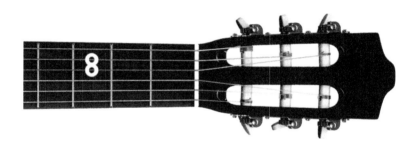

Secondary *Check Interval*: A - E Perfect Fifth
(harmonic pitch 5th string, 7th fret)

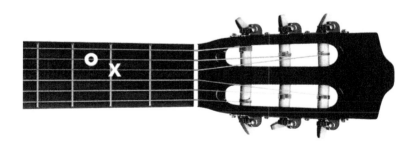

Check Interval: A - A Octave

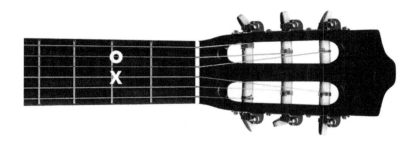

Check Interval: B - B Octave

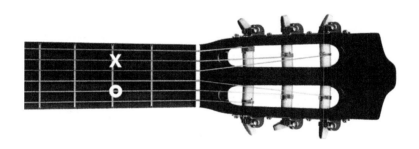

Check Interval: C - C Octave

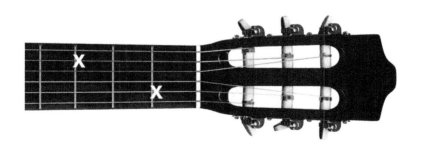

99

Check Interval: C - G Perfect Fifth

(Harmonic Pitch 3rd String, 12th Fret)

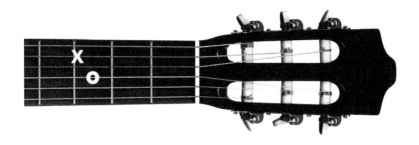

Check Interval: A - C#, Major Tenth

(harmonic pitch same as stopped C#)

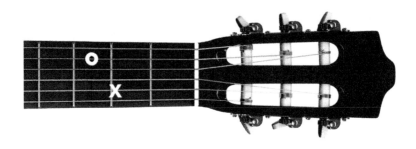

Why not just also tune the A string to the tuning fork?

Of course you can tune the A string to the tuning fork if you are beginning your tuning sequence on the A string. But here, having already set the D string to the fork, the rest of the strings have to be tuned according to the guitar, if the guitar is to sound at its best.

We may conceive a guitar note or string pitch to be a simple, single thing, like the tone of a tuning fork appears to be. But in actuality, every note of the guitar is a complex thing, cooked up from a whole recipe of many sound ingredients. Because of this, as far as possible, the guitar needs to be "tuned to itself".

*

The only open string interval available in this sequence, for tuning the A string, is the open perfect fourth on the 4th and 5th strings. So this, technically, is the tuning interval, but it's not the one we are most concerned with. We are going to be concerned with other intervals, and if we get these right, the open string fourth will turn out just fine.

The fast beating check for this string is the major tenth check, A (open string) to C# (2nd string, 2nd fret). The theoretical beat rate for this interval is about 4.5 beats per second. It should not beat faster than this. It beats *wide*, so as the A string is lowered the beat rate speeds up, or as the A string is raised, the beat rate slows down.

Method

Lower the A string, until the open perfect fourth between the A string and the D string is clearly beating too wide.

Now raise the A string, tuning the open fourth with the D string, until it is left wide with about one beat per second.

Check the major tenth A (open) - C# (2nd string, 2nd fret). We are aiming for 4-5 beats per second in this interval. If it sounds too fast, then raise the A string a little more, listening to the open fourth, and then check the major tenth again. If it sounds too slow, drop the A string again, and bring it up until the major tenth sounds right.

101

When you think you have the right beat rate in the major tenth, then it's time to do some checks.

Check the octave A (open) - A (3rd string, 2nd fret), *and* the perfect fifth C (A-string, 3rd fret) - G (open). *These work as a pair*, but they *oppose each other*. In other words, as one gets better (slower beating), the other gets worse (faster beating) and *vice versa*.

If there is no stopping sharp on the strings, then when the octave A-A is perfectly tuned, the perfect fifth C-G will beat with only one beat every two seconds. If there is some stopping sharp, then we're going to have to come to a compromise between the octave A-A and the perfect fifth C-G. Either way, uses the same method.

If the beat rate in the major tenth sounds about right (4-5 beats), then the perfect fifth C-G and the octave A-A should checked against each other. If the strings are stopping sharp, then the octave will be just a tiny amount wide, and the fifth will be beating narrow. It could be up to around 2 beats per second, but very likely will be less than that.

If the beat rate in the major tenth is actually too fast, then the octave will sound too bad (too much beating), and the perfect fifth too good (not enough beating compared to what it could take).

If the beat rate in the major tenth is too slow, then the octave will sound good, but the perfect fifth will be beating too fast.

Remember:

- As we lower the A string, the major tenth gets faster, the octave gets worse (more beating), and the perfect fifth get better (i.e. less beating).

- As we raise the A string, the major tenth get slower, the octave gets better (less beating), and the perfect fifth gets worse (more beating).

So now we listen to that opposing pair of intervals, the perfect fifth C-G and the octave A-A.

It's perfectly in order to *expect* the octave to always sound a little better than the perfect fifth, because perfect fifths are *meant* to be tempered, and octaves aren't. The reason we may be about to *compromise* the octave (if we have to) is because of *stopping sharp* on the strings, which is due to inharmonicity.

If you think the perfect fifth sounds too fast, then this should be confirmed by the major tenth being too slow.

If you think the perfect fifth sounds too slow, then this should be confirmed by the major tenth being too fast.

So briefly, good technique looks like this:

Tune the A string up from flat on the open fourth, and with each small raise, check the <u>octave A-A</u>, the <u>fifth C-G</u>, in that order. Each time you hear the octave needs to be better, you listen to the fifth to make sure it can take some more beating, and you go back to open fourth to tune up a fraction more. This cycling through checks and tuning should sound like you are playing a repeated, three-chord phrase, with tuning up on the third chord each time, (the open fourth).

When the octave and the fifth are both OK, then check the major tenth. If it's 4 - 5 beats per second, everything is fine. Otherwise you've got something on the wrong side and you need to start this string again. The octave C-C (A string, 3rd fret, to B string, 1st fret), should now be fine.

5: The 1st string (E)

Tuning Interval: **B - E Perfect Fourth**
(harmonic pitch 1st string, 7th fret)

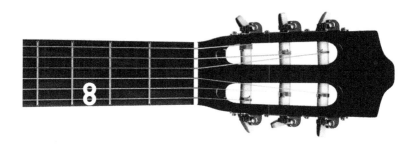

Tuning Interval: **A - E Perfect Twelfth**
(harmonic pitch 5th string, 7th fret)

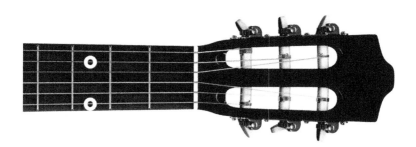

Check Interval: D - F#, Major Tenth

(harmonic pitch same as stopped F#)

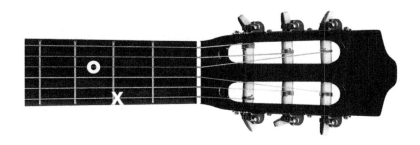

Check Interval: B - F#, Perfect Fifth

(harmonic pitch 2nd string, 7th fret)

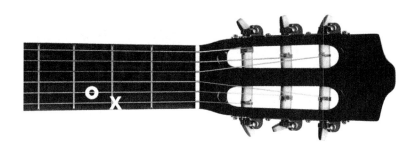

Check Interval: E - E Octave

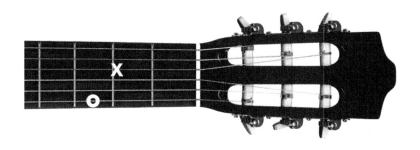

Check Interval: F - F Octave

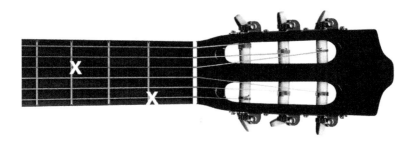

Check Interval: G - G Octave

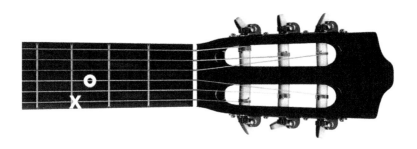

The 1st string can now be tuned to the harmonic over the 7th fret of the A string (no beating).

The fast beating interval we are going to set is the major tenth D (open string) to F# on the 1st string. The theoretical beat rate for this interval is **5.9** beats per second.

So we are going to set this to *the same beat rate as the open major sixth* D - B (the open strings). If you remember, the pitch of the harmonic to listen for, when tuning the major sixth D - B, is the one over the 7th fret of the 2nd string (B). This pitch is an F#. We need to listen to precisely the same pitch harmonic in the sound of the major tenth D - F# that we are about to tune.

So having got the pitch of the harmonic to listen for, play the open major sixth D - B, and listen to the beat rate. The beauty of this check is that both the pitch and the beat rate of the harmonic is the same in both intervals. You just compare the D - F# with the D - B, and make sure it the same.

You may find after tuning the 1st string to the harmonic on the 5th string, that this turns out right, at first try. If not, you'll need to lower the open E and then bring it up against the harmonic again.

There are two octave checks to make on this. The first is G (open 3rd string) - G (1st string, 3rd fret). The second is E (4th string, 2nd fret) - E (open 1st string). Both octaves should be good. If they are, you'll find the octave check F - F is good, too.

Generally, you should find that tuning the open E to the 5th string harmonic initially, gets you at least very close to where you need to be. Running through the checks G - G, E - E, and D - F#, playing them like a tune, should tell you if you need to go back and alter the 1st string a tiny amount, using the harmonic on the 5th string. If the octaves are slightly off, the tenth D - F# will tell you whether you need to raise or lower the E string.

6: The 6th string (E)

Tuning Interval: **E - E Double Octave**

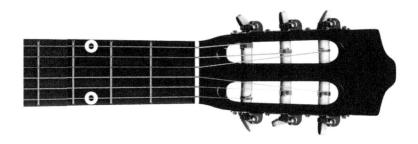

Check Interval: **E - G# Major Tenth**

(harmonic pitch same as stopped G)

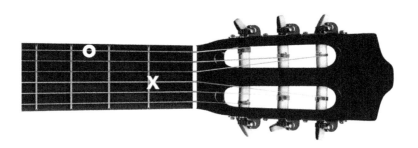

Check Interval: **G - G Octave**

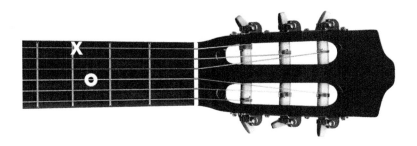

Check Interval: **E - E Octave**

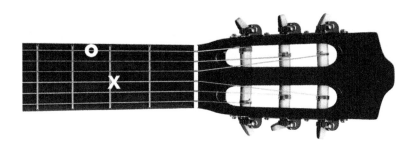

The tuning interval for the 6th string is the double octave with the 1st string. The other single octaves G-G and E-E (see above) must also sound good.

The other important check is the major tenth E (open 6th) - G# (3rd string, 1st fret).

The tenth is a wide, fast-beating interval, with a theoretical beat rate of around 3 beats per second. Anything faster that this will tend to be detrimental to the intonation in E major, and this is something that many guitarists are very sensitive to.

Being stopped on the third string, the G# does run the risk of stopping considerably sharp, which will increase the beat rate. Excessive beating in this interval is very clear on the guitar, and if it is not as slow as possible, it can spoil the sound of the E major chord. Using this tuning method we can usually achieve the Equal Temperament 3 beats per second in this interval.

Inharmonicity in the 3rd string can cause dispersion in the string's partials, sufficiently away from a true harmonic series, to make the perceived musical pitch of the stopped G# sound higher than expected, *even when we have the correct beat rate*. (Our "brain's perception" of musical pitch is affected by the frequency relationships between the partials).

If you are tempted to have this beat rate slower than Equal Temperament, then there is some room for manoeuvre on the E (6th) string, by raising it a little. But there will be a payoff in the octaves, especially the octave G-G.

Don't be tempted to lower the 3rd string, unless you have checked the open major third G - B, and found that it is not beating fast enough.

Generally speaking, making random changes to the tuning to correct isolated intervals is not a good idea. It's better to check through the whole set of strings from the beginning. Once really familiar with the tuning setup, the root of any errors in the tuning can usually be very quickly found.

Checking the octave E (open) - E (2nd fret on the D string)

If you find this E-E won't work out when the 6th string is a good double octave with the 1st string, then either the D string has moved, or the B string has moved.

It's easy enough to check the D string again with the fork or other reference source. If the B string has moved, you will hear it in the beat rate of the open sixth D - B, which will now not be as expected (it should be at about 6 beats per second).

If you have to alter the B string again, you'll also have to run through the tuning of the other three strings again, before getting back to the E, 6th string.

Equal Temperament in Tablature

The beat rates given in the following tablature are the theoretical predictions from "traditional" theory. This takes no account of inharmonicity, stopping sharp, or false beating.

The rates are given to one decimal place but *this is purely academic*. All the rates for the slow beating intervals, perfect fourths and perfect fifths, are indicative only, of what will happen in practice. The same is true for the concept of "0 beats" for the octaves.

Remember that we are aiming to get the *fast beating* interval beat rates right, and to get the best compromise between the other intervals.

This is because letting the fast beating intervals end up compromised, as a result of tuning only slow beating intervals, fails to get the best compromise in the slow beating intervals themselves.

Stage 1: 4th string

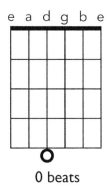

0 beats

Stage 2: 2nd string

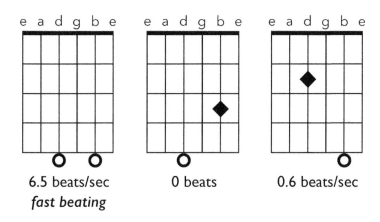

6.5 beats/sec
fast beating

0 beats

0.6 beats/sec

113

Stage 3: 3rd string

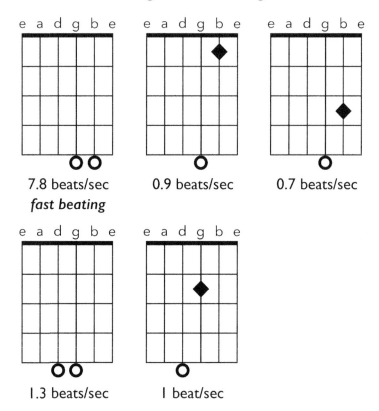

7.8 beats/sec
fast beating

0.9 beats/sec

0.7 beats/sec

1.3 beats/sec

1 beat/sec

Stage 4: 5th string

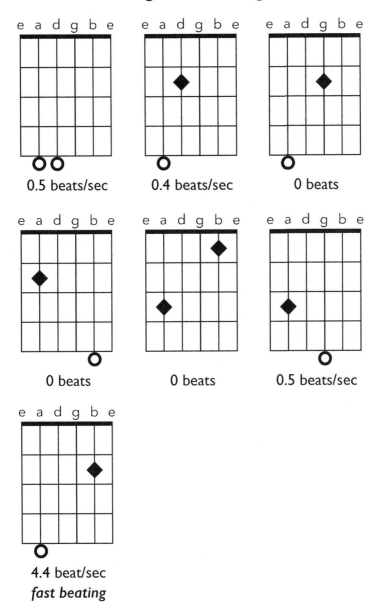

0.5 beats/sec   0.4 beats/sec   0 beats

0 beats   0 beats   0.5 beats/sec

4.4 beat/sec
fast beating

115

Stage 5: 1st string

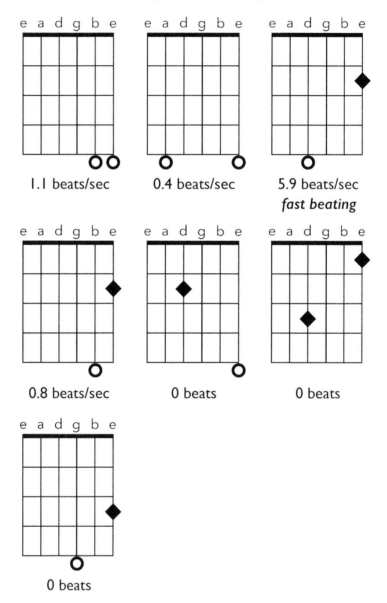

1.1 beats/sec

0.4 beats/sec

5.9 beats/sec
fast beating

0.8 beats/sec

0 beats

0 beats

0 beats

Stage 6: 6th string

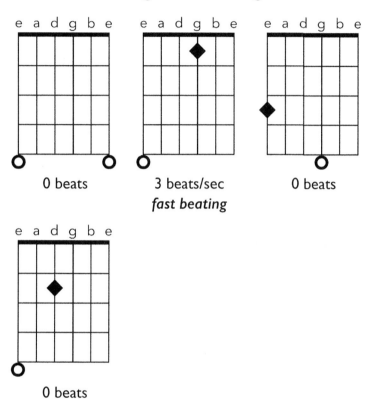

Non Standard Pure Tunings

The standard 6-string guitar tuning

6	5	4	3	2	1
E	A	D	G	B	E

is not the only one in use. There are many others, and the general principle in deviating from the standard tuning is to change the position of the open double octave, or, more commonly, to replace it with an open octave or introduce more open octaves.

Perhaps the simplest such change is tuning the 6th string down a tone to D:

6	5	4	3	2	1
D	A	D	G	B	E

But we can also go all the way into an open string tuning that in itself forms a basic chord. Probably the most obvious example that requires *lowered* string tensions is *open D tuning*:

6	5	4	3	2	1
D	A	D	F#	A	D

Tunings such as this, which increase the number of open string octaves, often also increase the resonance of the instrument, especially where they involve lowering of string tensions.

Other examples involving raised tensions are the open E tuning:

6	5	4	3	2	1
E	B	E	G#	B	E

and the open G (second inversion) tuning:

6	5	4	3	2	1
D	G	D	G	B	D

The open D tuning creates a D major chord on the open strings. Similarly, open E create an E major chord, and open G creates a second inversion G major chord on the open strings.

As long as you want to base your harmony around the key of the tuning, then this has obvious advantages in simplifying fingering in the left-hand.

In Equal Temperament tuning a pure (beatless) octave can be divided into a wide-tempered perfect fourth, and a narrow tempered perfect fifth.

A pure octave also divides into a pure perfect fourth and a pure perfect fifth. Tunings with multiple open octaves with perfect fourths or fifths in between, work best with pure intervals.

So the best principle to adopt in tuning such as this, is simply to tune everything pure (beatless) using just the open strings.

Where there is an open string major third, as there is here, the sweetness of a pure major third can really be exploited. There will be in general, always a mismatch between stopped notes and open strings, but in the context of how such tunings are used, this doesn't matter, and is usually hidden by the sheer resonance of the open strings.

In open D tuning, the use of the *barre* in left hand fingering to create, say, *G Maj, F# Maj,* and *A Maj* chords (*A Maj, G# Maj* and *B Maj* in open E tuning, and *G Maj, B Maj* and *D Maj* in open G tuning), may change the intonation due to stopping sharp on the strings, but this isn't generally enough to worry about.

The 2nd Fret Method

This is a brief, quick tuning method for Equal Temperament that takes account of stopping sharp, using the second fret.

It may not be as thorough as the previous Equal Temperament method, but it is very quick, and gives a good result.

The instructions assume that you can now think about two or three intervals at once, and how they affect each other, when they are interconnected, or work against each other.

The perfect fifths may be up to 2 beats per second narrow, depending on how sharp strings are stopping. Theoretically they would be much slower than this, and if they are working out this fast, you can only have them slower, if you accommodate it by compromising your octaves more.

- Begin by tuning the D string to your reference source.

- Now tune the B string so the major sixth with the D string, at 6 - 7 beats per second. Check the octave D (open) - D (2nd string, 3rd fret), and the perfect fifth E (on the D string) - B (open). They'll work against each other. Cycle through all three intervals, adjusting the B string accordingly.

- Tune the A string to the D string as a tempered open fourth (a little wide, about one beat per second). Now check the major tenth A - C# (on the B string) and the octave B (on the A string) - B (open). The octave should be good, and the tenth should be 4 to 5 beats per second. Adjust accordingly.

- Tune the G string as an open fourth to the D string (about one beat wide). Check the octave A (open) to A (on the G string), and the perfect fifth C (on the A string) - G (open). The octave should be good, and the fifth should be tempered (narrow). They'll work against each other. Always retune on the open fourth.

- Tune the 1st string as an open twelfth from the A string. Check the major tenth D (open) - F# (on the 1st string), and the octave E (on the D string) - E (open 1st string). The octave should be good and the tenth the same beat rate as the open sixth D - B. Adjust accordingly.

- Tune the 6th string a double octave from the 1st string. Check the single octave E (open) - E (on the D string), the octave G (on the 6th string) - G (open), and the major tenth E (open 6th string) - G# (on the G string). The octaves should be good, and the major tenth beating at no more than 3 beats per second.

If you are now familiar with the general way to approach guitar tuning issues, and have a grasp of *stopping sharp* works with temperament on the guitar, you might want to work out your own variation. You might want to create a completely new method that addresses some unique issue on your own guitar, or in some particular music.

Printed in Great Britain
by Amazon

62513213R00070